RIDE WITH THE DEVIL

RIDE WITH THE DEVIL
James Schamus

ff

faber and faber

First published in 1999
by Faber and Faber Limited
3 Queen Square London WC1N 3AU
Published in the United States by Faber and Faber, Inc.,
a division of Farrar, Straus and Giroux, Inc., New York

Photoset by Parker Typesetting Service, Leicester
Printed in England by Mackays of Chatham plc, Chatham, Kent

A CIP record for this book
is available from the British Library

ISBN 0–571–20163–6

2 4 6 8 10 9 7 5 3 1

CONTENTS

Thanks to Ted Hope, David Linde, Anne Carey, Bob Colesberry and the entire team at Good Machine.

J. S.

Director Ang Lee

FOREWORD
Ang Lee

I grew up in Taiwan, where older people always complained that kids are becoming Americanized – they don't follow tradition and so we are losing our culture. As I got the chance to go around a big part of the world with my films, I heard the same complaints. It seems so much of the world is becoming Americanized. And when I read the book *Woe to Live On*, on which we based our movie, I realized the American Civil War was, in a way, where it all started. It was where the Yankees won not only territory but, in a sense, a victory for a whole way of life and of thinking.

The Yankee invasion has not only a surface meaning – Yankees continue to win militarily and economically – but also an internal meaning. It changes you, in a kind of unstoppable way. Everyone is equal, everyone has the right to fulfill themselves – this is the Yankee principle. Now we must study ourselves, our personalities, in order to know how best to be fulfilled – this is all very modern, and so is the new social order based on that. Along with this, we learn to respect other people's freedom, too, even as we lose a certain connection to tradition.

This is what the Civil War meant to me – and I think it meant this as well to the boys in the movie, who are also non-Yankees. So the Civil War is not only on the surface, of blood and guts, it is also a personal war that leads to the new world in which we are living today – the world of democracy and capitalism.

The story starts with the Southern boys' point of view; the perspective of those who will lose to the Yankees. But then it gradually changes to focus on the points of view of the two outsiders – the German immigrant and the black slave – as well as that of the young woman. Through them we come to experience the changes that freedom will bring. It is their emancipation that the film becomes about, their coming of age. So, as a Taiwanese, I can identify with the Southerners as the Yankees change their way of life for ever, but I also identify more strongly with these outsiders, who grasp at freedom, and fight for it.

On the Missouri-Kansas border was the frontier of America

before the Civil War. The border not just between North and South, but between the settled country and the wild, wild West. Yet today it is the center of the country. The Big Muddy river that divided the two frontier states was where Mark Twain sailed his steamboat up and down, soon to create a pure American kind of literature. So our story is about the very heart of America, even as this heart was – and still so often is – torn apart by racial and other conflicts. Even as America seems to conquer the world with the promise of freedom, it has still not fully conquered itself, or achieved its own freedom. This ongoing struggle and hope is expressed through the film.

Overall, making the film was a very enjoyable working experience. Especially the local enthusiasm in Kansas and Missouri, and the devotion and work of the young actors I got a chance to work with. Pattonsburg, the town where we shot the Lawrence massacre sequence, was a very moving place. The local people were in the process of moving because of big floods to a new town they were building, so we were able to inherit their old town from them. They worked to help build the sets over their old houses for three or four months, then played extras, and then watched their old town burn down. The men played at being slaughtered; the women at trying to save them. The whole experience was very moving and surreal at the same time – something that could only have happened while making a film.

FRAGMENTS TOWARDS AN INTRODUCTION
James Schamus

For three films in a row – *Sense and Sensibility*, *The Ice Storm* and now *Ride with the Devil* – Ang Lee has worked from screenplays adapted from novels, and not simply novels, but 'literary' novels. This puts his work in something of the much-maligned 'cinema of quality' tradition, that body of 'classy' Hollywood movies that borrows its middlebrow legitimacy from its literary pedigree. Shall we disown, with a measure of embarrassment, this lineage? Or proudly reclaim it, ironically, as hipper than any heroin-injected, sideways-revolver-pointing pop entertainment could be?

Adaptation: not the transposition of story from one medium to another, but the transmission and transformation of one form of cultural work into other populations and markets.

Novels want you to be alone. Movies want you to be alone *en masse*. Novelizations and screenplay tie-in books want you to be *en masse* while alone.

Novels display the expense of an individual labor. Movies display the expense of huge sums of capital. Contemporary fine arts display the ways in which display itself can create value without the help of either labor or capital. Novels and movies are old-fashioned by comparison.

Hollywood, contrary to informed opinion, does not need novelists for its stories – Hollywood has need of only a few stories, and it already owns them. When a film studio buys the rights to a book, it is buying not a story but a set of architectural floor plans from which it can build unique-looking sets into which it will let loose a couple of movie stars who will bump into each other and get into 'situations' on their inevitable way to the bedroom. Interesting movies happen when the floor plans are so elaborate or so impossible to build that the characters get lost in the hallways or locked in the bathrooms and are forced to fight their ways back into the story that Hollywood thought it was making.

What, then, did Daniel Woodrell, the author of the novel *Woe to Live On*, on which we based our movie, sell us when he sold us 'the rights' to his book? The story? The characters? The settings? Surely not the words he had written, the words that make up the specific music of his art, his *writing*. Perhaps what we bought was a kind of cultural mineral rights, exploitable only by stripping Woodrell's novel of its words.

Among the things Woodrell did sell us was the use of the title of his book. But, as one studio president put it, 'I'm not spending millions of dollars on a movie with the word *Woe* in the title.'

Woodrell's novel is at once intensely literary and wonderfully cinematic. But its cinematic immediacy made it, oddly, all the more difficult to adapt. On the one hand was the guilty pleasure of simply transcribing whole scenes in the book from novel into screenplay format with hardly a change in comma placement. On the other hand, there was the glaring structural problem of how to glue those scenes together without the help of Woodrell's writing, the words that held the world of the novel together. Consider Jake's wonderful rumination on his lost finger, which, he muses, will make his future rotting corpse identifiable, thus sparing his father the torture of 'uncertain wonders' about his fate. In the script reprinted here, we followed that speech with a scene, also lifted nearly straight from the book, of unspeakable brutality, as the Union prisoners are tortured and killed the following morning. In the book, the almost hallucinatory violence of Jake's existence flows naturally in the river of language that embeds his experience, even as he begins to rebel against the brutality around him. But in the first cut of the film, the violence appeared more as a simple, shocking juxtaposition, as if we were staging the relationship between language and action in conflict, as two opposed orders of existence – precisely what the book avoided. The scene was dropped from the film, as we constructed the sequence more tightly around the story of Jake's inadvertent abetting of his father's murder. A more strictly 'narrative' approach than the novel's more experiential logic.

Woe to Live On is in some ways a celebration of the intertwining of American writing and American speech, of the way, since

Huckleberry Finn especially (written by Woodrell's fellow Missourian Mark Twain, né Samuel Clemens), American literary prose hears itself in dialogue with transcribed, unschooled, spoken vernacular. But, ironically, when you pull that speech off of the written page and throw it up on the screen, the results can often be oddly 'literary' – a quality we carefully embraced in the screenplay.

The so-called (white) literary establishment had, for a long time, understood America as having two literatures: American literature and Southern literature. (Somehow, we never had a 'Northern' literature.) In his novel, Woodrell stages the battle between the American and the Southern both literally and figuratively and, like Twain (the Northern literary professional) and Clemens (the Southern raconteur), he knowingly resolves the North/South conflict by, in the end, resolutely facing *West*. We took Twain's and Woodrell's cue in the movie, making the last image of the film the archetypal first image of the Western: a lone horseman riding under the big sky of the prairie frontier. (Of course, in this version of the myth, the horseman is an armed black man heading south . . .)

The movie is, thus, a kind of ur-Western, a rereading of the myth of the West in light of the violent racial and regional and sexual politics that informed it. Think of the century's first and most influential Western novel, itself adapted many times to the screen, Owen Wister's *The Virginian* (1903). It is emphatically about a Southerner, written by a somewhat neurasthenic Northerner (Owen went West on the recommendation of the family doctor, the now notorious S. Weir Mitchell, whose infamous 'rest cure' helped inspire Charlotte Perkins Gilman's classic early feminist work *The Yellow Wallpaper*), and it is fixated on issues of race and racial 'purity'. (Teddy Roosevelt was a friend of Wister's from their Harvard days and a fan of the novel's racial politics.) The novel projects its racial agenda into the mythical figure of the cowboy (even the Indians are more or less extinct by the time Wister helps invent the 'West'), as the Virginian (we never learn his name) uses his naturally aristocratic Southern bearing to bring rough justice to a wild West, reluctantly leading, in the book's climax, a lynch mob that kills a gang of rustlers that includes among its half-breeds and Mexicans the Virginian's former best friend. In Wister's vision, the legacy of the Civil War is given closure by bringing Northern and Southern whites together (the Virginian eventually marries the Northern schoolteacher who was at first violently opposed to the lynching), in order to unify all whites in battle against the *real* losers of the conflict: blacks and other 'foreigners'[1]. *Ride with the Devil* is a modest attempt to regraft on to the history of the Western this racially charged back-story.

It is also an entertainment, a myth for sale.

1 This is also the vision of the dominant American political culture. See Anthony Marx's *Making Race and Nation* (Cambridge, 1998) for an illuminating historical and comparative overview.

NOTES TO THE SCRIPT

What you will read here is the shooting script with which we commenced production of the film. The completed film is significantly changed, mainly because of a number of trims and ellisions, made for the usual reasons: pacing, clarity, accidents of fate. I'll touch on some, but not all, of the more exemplary changes below.

1. The opening sequence, a kind of 'preamble' set before the war's commencement, was created for the film in an attempt to give some sense of what antebellum life was like for Jake and Jack Bull. It also allowed us some breathing room for explaining a little of the confusing historical and political background of the film, as the movie doesn't present the usual image of the Civil War, of easily identifiable hordes of gray- and blue-clad soldiers clashing on the field of honor in the fight either for or against slavery. What to make of a state like Missouri, slave-holding but officially pro-Union, already in something of a state of war with its anti-slavery neighbors next-door in Kansas? Many Missourians were pro-Union but distrustful of the North; others were radical Confederates. And many, especially in the western part of the state, had suffered for the five years leading up to the Civil War at the hands of marauding groups of 'Jayhawkers' from Kansas, often no more than criminals pretending to be abolitionists, who raided farms and 'liberated' them of slaves and horses. (Of course, Missouri itself sent into Kansas its own 'Border Ruffians' to do the same to the newly arrived Northern settlers.)

Then there was the specific outlook of the German immigrants, such as Jake's father, who had settled in Missouri during the late '40s and early '50s, most of whom were radical '48-ers' – men and women who had fled Germany after the failed 1848 revolution there – and who were violently opposed to slavery. These Germans – Deutschmen, erroneously called 'Dutchmen' by the Southerners (hence Jake's nickname of 'Dutchy') – were crucial Northern allies in Missouri, and were especially loathed by pro

Confederate Missourians. So, Jake's brief encounter with his father at the beginning of the movie is not simply about parental anxiety, as there is a strong political undercurrent to his father's nervousness about the war. Jake's siding with Jack Bull is a noteworthy defection from his father's community.

Once the war got underway, Missouri ended up as something of an American Vietnam, occupied by Union forces and under martial law during most of the conflict, with local populations giving support and cover to loosely organized gangs of Southern 'Bushwhackers'. These guerillas terrorized Union sympathizers and preyed on Northern patrols and supply lines, often surprising their enemies by impersonating Union troops. As the war dragged on, they became increasingly desperate and bloodthirsty, devolving eventually into criminal gangs that had little interest in or regard for the politics of the conflict that spawned them. The most famous of them, William Quantrill, was himself an Ohioan who posed as a Southerner. He plays a brief but crucial role later in the film.

How to get enough of this information into the first few minutes of the film without making the movie seem like a high-school history lecture? We wrote the debate that takes place at the wedding as a dramatic way to get the history in, but, ironically, the more of it we cut into the movie and screened to test audiences during the film's editing, the more people were confused. Only later, during post-production, did we think to take out most of the debate, and replace it with an explanatory 'crawl' at the beginning of the film, which explained simply who the Jayhawkers and the Bushwhackers were. We also added a voice-over narration, in the form of a letter from Jake to Jack Bull's mother, that explains how the boys ended up as Bushwhackers. The goal was not to make everything absolutely clear within the first five minutes – a relative impossibility, and not necessary in any case – but rather to give enough information to the audience so that it could continue to watch the film without too much anxiety over who was who and what was what.

By the by, these first scenes of the film were in fact the last scenes shot, both for weather purposes (we shot from early spring into summer, with a few shots taken during pre-production in the snow, so that we could pretend to have all four seasons in the film), but, even more importantly, for reasons of facial hair continuity. Our Bushwhackers wore their hair long and sported a variety of facial hair styles, and rather than have our actors paste on mustaches and don wigs every morning (a process that often can take hours, and one which often results in violent allergic reactions to the various glues used), we simply let them grow their hair out during pre-production, shaping it and adding bits and pieces here and there as we went along. Then, at the end of the film, we cleaned Tobey and Skeet up for the first and final scenes of the film.

3. One reason Tobey Maguire is so bright and fresh in this scene is that he had a 104 degree fever the day we shot it: after nearly five straight months of grueling sixteen-hour days on the film, Ang admitted he'd finally ground his hard-working lead actor more or less into the Missouri mud.

21. Would a black man have been found fighting with the Bushwhackers? It is a little known fact that a small number of free and slave African-Americans fought on the side of the Confederacy during the war, and their stories are among the most fascinating of the period. We studied a number of sources Woodrell had used to create Holt's character, including an oral history transcript of John Nolan, who served as a spy and scout for the infamous Bushwhacker William Quantrill. These men had a variety of reasons for joining the fight on the side of the South. Some wanted to prove to white Southerners that blacks could be as loyal and trustworthy as whites, in the hope that after the war, if the South won, the treatment of blacks would improve. Some were fiercely loyal to white friends or masters, whom they often served as man-servants. Others saw service in the war as a welcome relief from the drudgery of plantation life. And probably for the vast majority, being near the front lines meant being that much nearer the North – and when they got the chance, they crossed the lines and joined forces with the Union army.

Some of them performed in active combat duty, though this was rare. But there are numerous accounts of armed blacks fighting for the South, although, politically, Southern leaders were loath to admit their presence in the ranks, no matter how small. Most often, though, blacks served as laborers, valets or teamsters. Many in the South were afraid to arm large numbers of blacks, though by the end of the war, even the President of the Confederacy was admitting that arming blacks was the only way the South had a chance to win. It's often been said that if the South had armed its blacks earlier, it might indeed have won. Ironically, it was wealthy Southern slave-owners who were the most vociferous in their arguments against blacks being mustered into active battle duty – they were worried about their valuable property being killed in action.

Presenting a character in Holt's situation was something we didn't take lightly. For one thing, there's the fear that such stories as his can be used incorrectly by apologists for the Confederate regime and for the institution of slavery, to argue: 'See, slavery wasn't so bad – even blacks fought for the South.' And, in fact, there are so-called 'revisionists' who do appear to argue something of the sort. The film counters such nonsense not by shying away from presenting what is obviously an exceptional story, but by taking that story as the occasion to chart how even the exceptions prove the bitter rule of slavery's legacy. By recovering and interpreting the life stories of these often heroic men, we can understand better the emotional and political realities they faced and how they dealt with them.[2]

27. This is one of three particularly painful cuts that were made simply for pacing and length. Skeet is simultaneously menacing and sympathetic here – a remarkable performance, played against a bravura turn by Sean Whalen, who played the part of Clark. Also missing from the finished film is the scene at Claude Daily's house after the shoot-out. The great Broadway performer and clown Bill Irwin played the part of the ever-drunker Daily, whose wild dance around the whiskey jug is a marvel of sloppy precision and restrained slapstick. And, third, we cut young Riley's death scene after Holt and Jake return to the gang from the Brown farm. When Thomas Guiry auditioned for the role, he read the scene, and there were tears in Ang's and casting director Avy Kaufman's

2 There's a great deal of exciting scholarship that's leading the way to this new understanding. See Ervin L. Jordan's *Black Confederates and Afro-Yankees in Civil War Virginia* (Charlottesville, 1995), especially the chapter entitled 'Zealots of the Wrong: Afro-Confederate Loyalism' for an excellent recent overview.

eyes when it was over. It was even more moving on film – but the ruthless need to stay 'on story' at that point forced its removal. One hopes that the eventual DVD of the film will include these scenes.

57. While we dropped in the editing room Jake's question about how Holt knows how to talk, we preserved the sense of surprise that greets Holt's wry 'coming out' into language. Nearly silent, if not quite invisible, during the movie's first half, Holt emerges as Jake's equal and the movie's co-hero by the end. Negotiating the character of Holt's voice, and his ever greater sense of self-expression, was no easy matter. His 'slave speech' couldn't be too wildly divergent from the linguistic world of the rest of the film, or it might ring out as shockingly stereotypical, replacing the content of his words with the sound of his enunciation. And yet it would be equally oppressive to silence the very sound and texture of what we might reasonably reconstruct as the historically accurate voice of lived slave experience. It's a conundrum faced by many interpreters of the slave era. Even, for example, the most progressive of educators often 'standardize' the spelling of slave oral histories, rather than reproduce the suspect 'dems' and 'disses' written down by the white interlocutors who transcribed (and often shaped) the slaves' stories. At the same time, one must acknowledge that such 'slave speech' stereotypes still, in some way, were responses to real and distinct linguistic performances that standardization erases. And, of course, the dialogue spoken by the white characters in the movie has itself been rigorously worked over, and, while historically inspired, can't be called historically accurate. To make the sole black character 'historically accurate' in this context would be to place him in a completely different linguistic universe, ejecting him from the world of the narrative Woodrell had fought so hard to make him central to.

The key for the film was therefore to find a linguistic meeting ground in which the historical and the literary could co-exist. Jeffrey Wright, who portrays Holt in the film, diligently, and with great erudition, trawled the historical records, and inflected much of his dialogue with the knowledge he gained. Jeffrey never lost sight of the fact that his is a performance in an essentially fictional work; but he also seized the opportunity to rehabilitate a way of speech-making almost never seriously voiced within the confines of the mass media, and he proved a tremendous collaborator in the creation of his character and of his character's language. Careful reading of his lines in the script against the finished film will reveal innumerable changes, all worked through painstakingly by Jeffrey, Ang and myself. Sometimes, historical accuracy would be compromised, especially in the early scenes when we wanted o give the audience time to acclimatize itself to Holt's speech. Other times, turns of phrase and verbal tags appear, coming directly from historical sources.

Compound all this with the fact that the character of Holt would have had to watch very carefully every word he said – a slight slip of the tongue could well have meant death – and you find another defining conflict in a character who, on the one hand, is finding his way to freedom and the power of self-articulation and, on the other hand, still needs to be perceived to be inarticulate and 'simple' by the whites around him. Wright's extraordinary performance manages delicately to balance all of these tensions.

You'll notice that all references to Sue Lee's horse are replaced with the word 'mule', an irony Jewel was particularly aware of, as she is a dedicated and accomplished equestrian who could outride any of the boys. She was a bit disappointed to hear that Ang wanted her on a mule in order to increase the humor of the situation.

The dugout set was built, along with the Brown house interiors, in a warehouse on the outskirts of Kansas City, and when you look out from inside the dugout you are looking at some purchased tree branches and a painted backdrop. Although most of the scenes in the dugout are supposed to take place in cold weather, in fact the set was unbearably hot, as we couldn't afford to air-condition the entire warehouse. Added to the heat were the sound problems; even a slight drizzle would turn the corrugated aluminium roof into a cacophonous percussion section, and, since we often used the warehouse as a 'cover' set when the weather was too bad to shoot outdoors, our sound mixer dreaded every minute there.

61. We had thought, once Jewel was cast in the film, that we should cut this sing-along, as we were worried that the singing

would break the illusion of this, Jewel's first acting role. But she is such a completely natural and convincing Sue Lee that we never gave it a second thought.

75. Slaves were often assigned Christian names by their masters, and assumed the last names of their masters. By telling Jake that Daniel is the name his mother gave him, Holt is sharing something that Jake would have understood to be quite significant – the identity that slavery and law had attempted to erase. For pacing reasons, we cut an earlier scene between Jake and Jack Bull that was meant to mirror this one, where Jake insists on Jack Bull calling him not by his nickname but by his 'real' name.

109. The Lawrence Massacre of August, 1863, in which guerilla leader William Quantrill led a hastily assembled group on what many thought would be a suicide mission into Kansas, is often called the greatest massacre in American history. Estimates vary on the number of Lawrence's citizens killed in the few hours Quantrill and his men spent in the town, but the number was certainly more than 180.

Many of the Southerners who rode with Quantrill that day were farmers and other non-combatants who were disgusted by the carnage and quietly refused to participate. But among the riders was also a hard core of Bushwhackers, who, while fighting on the Southern side, seem to have had few loyalties above and beyond their own criminal predilections. Indeed, Quantrill's gang proved to be a fertile training ground for the men who would become, after the Civil War was over, the West's most notorious criminals, including the Younger Brothers and the James Gang. In fact, Coleman Younger and Frank James participated in the Lawrence Raid; Jesse James has often been placed in Lawrence, too, but he was only fourteen at the time. He joined Quantrill's gang the following year.

The film's re-creation of the massacre was shot just a few miles from the James brothers' birthplace in western Missouri, in the small town of Pattonsburg, or at least what remained of Pattonsburg after the Federal Emergency Management Agency took the extraordinary step, after the historic 1993 floods, of ordering the town and its occupants to be moved to higher ground. As Ang recalls in his Preface, working in the town was an extraordinary event. It came about when the film's locations team and producer Bob Colesberry heard that FEMA was planning on demolishing the town, and offered to step in and do the job for them. After months of negotiations with various federal, state and local agencies, and with the citizens of the town, we landed the job, thus saving the expense of having to build and then burn down an entirely fake Lawrence. Designer Mark Friedberg and his crew dressed the town up with flats that covered existing buildings, and even moved houses around to fit the various shots that were planned. They were able to accomplish on a tight budget what would have otherwise cost millions to create, all with the help of local craftspeople and workers who transformed their hometown into a Hollywood back-lot, and then, dressed in period clothing, watched it all burn down.

Quantrill's speech here was radically rewritten during production to deflate its 'preacher' style and to replace it instead with something more wounded and personal, in keeping with our increased emphasis on the desperation of the Bushwhackers and the danger of our central characters who found themselves in their midst. We also took advantage of an extra day of 'pick-up' shooting on a sound stage in New York during the editing of the film (which we needed to get a shot of Tobey writing the letter he reads in voice-over at the beginning of the movie) to add some extra dialogue at the poker game in the camp, again stressing the danger of Quantrill's arrival. We intercut the new poker players into the scene, having dressed and bearded them to match our original players.

122. Not much of the elaborately scripted Lawrence sequence printed here ended up making its way into the film, either because it was not shot owing to time and budget contraints or simply because it was not used after we screened the first rough cut of the film – which clocked in at well over three hours. Each of the vignettes – from the man dressed in woman's clothing to the colorful chatter of Dulinski – was based on stories recounted by survivors of the massacre. But in the end, we opted to keep the sequence focused on our main characters, and on the mounting tensions caused by their quietly heroic refusal to participate in the slaughter.

140. Jim Caviezel, who plays Black John with such intense conviction, asked me about a wonderful line Black John says to Jake in the book that I had left out of this scene: 'Do not think you are a good man. The thought will spoil you.' I realized my mistake in dropping it. On screen, it now anchors the entire scene.

141. The battle scene after Lawrence is perhaps where we take our greatest liberties with the historical record, as Quantrill's raiders made it back to Missouri with a minimum of incident. Still, with the help of Riley Flynn, the expert leader of our Civil War re-enactors, Ang researched meticulously what would have been the most typical strategies used in such a skirmish. We wanted a scene that dramatically put Jake and Holt in the middle, assaulted from every side, and which also would afford them, amidst all the chaos, a cover for their escape. Woodrell's way of handling Jake's removal from the gang in the book is fabulous – Pitt takes a shot at Jake while he's in the woods relieving himself. But I think seeing such a scene on screen would have made it too comical.

208. There was an audible gasp on set the day Tobey appeared shorn of his beard and long hair. After months of physically arduous shooting. Tobey was transformed back into the beatific boy (with, of course, the devilish grin) with whom Ang and I had first been smitten when casting *The Ice Storm*. Although I rarely admitted it during the writing process, even to myself, I had written the part of Jake specifically for Tobey, knowing full well that he was not (yet) the major star we would probably be required to cast for the lead. A supportive studio (one of whose executives, Mary Parent, had been instrumental in the making of *Pleasantville*, which would soon establish Tobey as star material), and an ever-patient Tobey (who held on even as the film's schedule got pushed again and again) aligned the stars in our favor. I must say I have no idea how the film could work if Tobey were not its lead.

211. Pitt's phrase 'No shit, Dutchy' is probably anachronistic, but for some reason I loved the sound of it when I came across it in the book and refused to remove it. After casting the young Irish actor Jonathan Rhys Myers as Pitt, I took the opportunity to collapse another character from the first draft into his, giving Pitt a tragic destiny at the end of the film, and making more central his

role not just as the bad guy but as the embodiment of a kind of sinister but human fatalism. (And, of course, by cutting out the other character we saved money on additional housing, travel, etc.) There really was a Bushwhacker, by the way, who went back to his home town to have a last drink and be murdered.

We changed Holt's 'That's right, Jake' to the more non-committal 'All right' in post-production looping. Jeffrey pointed out rightly that his character would probably not have gone out of his way to approve of Jake's sparing Pitt, even if he understood it.

212. Here, I tried to bring to closure the gestural and verbal 'structures' that undergird much of the film: the importance of names and naming; Jake's nervousness around 'niggers with guns' and Holt's simple affirmation that his armed struggle might not yet be over; Holt's touching of his hat, freely, without the coercion he faced earlier in the dugout. Each small gesture in this final scene echoes and reinterprets an earlier one in the film.

In some ways, this 'gestural' closure to the film extends and develops an approach I have had from the beginning to writing for Ang, be it the raised arms of the father that end *The Wedding Banquet*, the simple serving of the soup that closes *Eat Drink Man Woman* , the repeated arrival at the train station of *The Ice Storm*. In each film, some very simple human gesture or phrase becomes (I hope) charged with a meaning and resonance that is specifically cinematic, in that it eludes a strictly thematic or verbal accounting. For *Ride with the Devil* the 'bigness' of the movie's final shot – as I mentioned earlier, we always wanted the final image of the film to be the quintessential first image of the Western genre – called for a delicacy and restraint to the human words and movements that are balanced against it. In the end, we, and the film's characters with us, are assumed into the larger world of history and myth that Holt's ride into the vast prairie symbolizes and that the film attempts, in its own modest way, to revise. In large measure that revision is constituted by an attention to and a respect for the sanctity of human gesture and communication – the hallmarks of Ang Lee's work as a film-maker.

Universal Pictures presents A Good Machine production.

MAIN CAST

JACK BULL CHILES	Skeet Ulrich
JAKE ROEDEL	Tobey Maguire
SUE LEE SHELLEY	Jewel
DANIEL HOLT	Jeffrey Wright
GEORGE CLYDE	Simon Baker
PITT MACKESON	Jonathan Rhys Meyers
BLACK JOHN	James Caviezel
RILEY CRAWFORD	Thomas Guiry
ORTON BROWN	Tom Wilkinson

CREW

Based on the novel	*Woe to Live on* by Daniel Woodrell
Screenplay by	James Schamus
Produced by	Ted Hope
	Robert F. Colesberry
	James Schamus
Directed by	Ang Lee
Associate Producer	Anne Carey
Executive Producer	David Linde
Casting Director	Avy Kaufman
Music Composer	Mychael Danna
Editor	Tim Squyres
Director of Photography	Frederick Elmes
Costume Designer	Marit Allen
Production Designer	Mark Friedberg

Ride with the Devil

1 EXT. COUNTRY ROAD – DAY

A lone horseman gallops wildly through the lush, empty countryside. The horse flies down the country road, expertly guided by its rider.

CLOSE ON: *we see he's a handsome, well-scrubbed youth, hovering between boy- and manhood. Neither exhilarated nor afraid, he exudes an aura of total control over the animal he rides.*

2 EXT. CHILESES' HOUSE – DAY

He rides past an ostentatious gate, to the rear of a handsome manor and outbuildings.

Four men stand by the gate, bored and hot. Each is armed – a shotgun, carbine, pistols tucked into their belts. They stand to on his approach, but relax, recognizing him, as he pulls back the reins on his horse.

> GUARD
>
> You're late, Dutchy.

Jake 'Dutchy' Roedel smiles, looking up to the house, around which are parked numerous wagons and buggies, tended to by four or five liveried slaves.

He dismounts and walks to the rear entrance of the house, greeting various slaves and workers with familiarity.

3 INT. CHILESES' HOUSE. LARGE PARLOR – DAY

A wedding is in progress. The Minister continues his speechifying as Sally Chiles stands, radiant in her white gown, across from young Horton Lee, Jr.

> MINISTER
> (*in background*)
>
> . . . Giver of all spiritual grace, the author of everlasting life, send thy blessing upon these thy servants, this man and this woman, whom we bless in thy name; that as Isaac and Rebecca lived faithfully together, so these persons may surely perform and keep the vow and covenant between them made . . .

Jake cautiously enters at the back of the crowded room, filled with fifty or so well-dressed Southern gentry. He sidles over to where his best friend Jack Bull Chiles leans against the rear wall. Jack Bull has an aristocratic and patrician air in his dandified and expensive suit and boots, which look all the more so next to Jake's more homespun attire.

Jake, sniffing the air, smiles ironically at his friend.

> JACK BULL
> (*whispering*)

What's ticklin' you?

> JAKE
> (*whispering*)

You smell something funny? It's like a New Orleans cathouse in here.

> JACK BULL

You fool. That's the eau-de-Cologne my ma slapped on me this morning.

Jake stifles a laugh as Jack Bull smacks the back of his head. The Minister drones on.

And what brings you so late to my sister's funer– I mean wedding?

> JAKE

Ah, my pa had me working.

Asa Chiles, his distinguished-looking father, gives the boys a look to quiet them down.

> ASA CHILES

Son.

They hush up as the ceremony continues.

4 EXT. CHILESES' HOUSE. PORCH – DAY

The boys join many of the older men, smoking and drinking, out on the porch. We hear dance music from the parlor inside. Among the men are Asa Chiles, Horton Lee, Sr, George Bowden and his son Alf, who nods to the boys as they enter.

ASA CHILES
(*looking down at the armed guards*)
You believe those men are necessary?

HORTON LEE, SR
We can take no further chances. Asa, you and I both know it
will soon be war between us and the Yankee aggressors. With
that Black Republican Abe Lincoln in the White House,
Missouri is no longer safe from the depredations of Jennison
and his Kansas Jayhawkers.

ASA CHILES
They have yet to strike this deep into Missouri, Horton.
Lawrence, Kansas and its abolitionists are a long way from here.

HORTON LEE, SR
But there are Union men even here among us, Asa. Schmitz
and his Germans form a militia at Independence. And his
Lawrence cohorts have eyes and ears among us – even here.

*There is an uncomfortable shuffling among the men. Alf Bowden gives
his father a look.*

GEORGE BOWDEN
If you refer to us Bowdens, Lee, you are sorely mistaken. We
may be Union men, yes. But we are Southerners too, and you
know well enough we'll have no hand in Jayhawking or
abolitionist provocations.

HORTON LEE, SR
I did not imply it, sir.

GEORGE BOWDEN
I believe, sir, you did.

ASA CHILES
Now, gentlemen, my home is no place and this is no time for
political quarrels. We are all old friends here.

*There is a brief silence. Everyone knows that with one more word, the
matter will be taken up by a duel. George Bowden breaks the silence.*

GEORGE BOWDEN
Asa Chiles, you have spoken truly. My apologies, Horton.

5

Whatever our beliefs, we are all in danger. These Jayhawkers may speak in the name of the Union, but they come only to plunder our property. In our will to defend our homes we are all united. I believe the Union should be preserved, and I fear for a general outbreak of war, but that doesn't make me a Yankee or a Lawrence abolitionist.

Horton Lee, Sr raises his glass, warily, to Bowden.

>   HORTON LEE, SR
> Well said, sir.

The boys trade glances.

5 EXT. CHILESES' HOUSE – DAY

Later. Sally Chiles gives her mother a tearful farewell hug and gets into a fine carriage with her new husband. Others in carriages and on horseback, accompanied by slaves in livery, are departing with the wedding party, accompanied by the armed guards.

Jake and Jack Bull wave goodbye from the porch.

>   JAKE
> I have been thinking, Jack Bull. A wedding is a peculiar thing.

>   JACK BULL
> It is no more peculiar, Jake, than slavery.

>   JAKE
> That is certain. And that is why I have often wondered for what cause those Northerners are so anxious to change our Southern institutions. For in both North and South men are every day enslaved at the altar, regardless of their state or color.

>   JACK BULL
> It is a type of subjugation. We shall avoid it, Jake.

>   JAKE
> Happily, my poverty ensures my freedom from such a fate.

>   JACK BULL
> Oh, not if my mother can help it. I heard her singing your praises earlier to the sister of the groom.

He nods towards a ruddy, pleasantly well-fed-looking young woman, who demurely looks his way as she is rather awkwardly helped into another carriage.

Asa and Mrs Chiles step back on to the porch to re-enter the house, passing the boys. Mrs Chiles smiles warmly at Jake.

JAKE

Good day, Mrs Chiles. Sir.

ASA CHILES

Please give my regards to your father. You know he is always invited –

JAKE

He's more comfortable working, you know –

MISSUS CHILES

You must at the least bring Mr Roedel some of the cake.

JAKE

I will, ma'am.

6 EXT. MILL – DAY

Jake walks up to the Chiles-owned millworks, a wrapped piece of cake in his hand.

7 INT. MILL – DAY

Jake enters and walks up the stairs to find his father, Otto Roedel, fixing some of the machinery.

> JAKE
>
> Father, Mrs Chiles sends her regards, and a piece of the cake.

> OTTO
> (*heavy German accent*)
> You are to see tomorrow Mrs Kreuzer.

Jake looks at him, puzzled.

> (*nodding to a broadsheet newspaper on the table*)
> The war – it is sure to come now with this secession. Mrs Kreuzer's husband will take you – in St Louis.

> JAKE
>
> Pa! I told you, I'm not goin' to huddle with all the other Lincoln-loving Germans in St Louis to –

> OTTO
>
> – It is safer! For us this is no war –

> JAKE
>
> – Pa. You may have borned me in Germany, but I was raised here. These are my people, and if it gets hot –

> OTTO
>
> Your people! No, Jake, this they are not. You will always be a Deutschman, a German, to them, no matter with who you are friends – Promise me you go to Mrs Kreuzer.

The old man walks, with some difficulty, to another piece of equipment and starts to work again, leaving Jake standing there, fuming.

8 INT. ROEDEL FARMHOUSE – NIGHT

Jake reads at the kitchen table from the light thrown off from a candle.

He looks and sees his father asleep in a small alcove in the corner.

A faint rumbling sound can be heard from outside.

It grows louder.

Jake furrows his brow. The sound grows nearer – the sound of a posse of horses riding quickly and hard. As Jake's father awakens, Jake blows out the candle and runs to the door. He stands in the doorway watching and listening.

9 EXT. ROEDEL FARMHOUSE – NIGHT

In the darkness, the horsemen, almost invisible, ride by without pausing. The sound of the horses grows fainter.

10 INT. ROEDEL FARMHOUSE – NIGHT

Jake spins around, finds his boots and starts to put them on. In the moonlight his father sits up and looks on, not saying a word.

11 EXT. ROAD – NIGHT

Jake rides cautiously, then dismounts, ties his horse and continues running along the roadside.

Jake approaches the drive to the Chileses' mansion. He pauses behind a stand of trees, bathed in a warm brown light.

12 EXT. CHILESES' HOUSE – NIGHT

From Jake's point of view, a macabre scene unfolds. Twelve horsemen circle around the front of the house. Fire pours from the downstairs windows on one side of the house.

The horsemen shout and holler as Mrs Chiles and a cluster of servants are held back.

A group of slaves stand silently, also under guard.

JAYHAWKER #1
(*to Mrs Chiles*)
Mrs Chiles – ma'am – you're gonna have to stand back there –

Suddenly there is a hurrah from around the side of the house as Asa Chiles is led, in his nightshirt, to the front drive.

JAYHAWKER #2
(*ad libs*)
We found 'im! Hidin' in the mill!

Obscured by the group, still from Jake's point of view, we see Asa being led to the front of the house. We see one of the horsemen raise and fire his pistol – there are four or five more shots.

On Jake, as he winces, involuntarily calling out.

Jake hears a branch crack behind him. He wheels around.

It's Jack Bull, shaking with fear and rage.

JACK BULL
Jake.

JAKE
(*whispering*)
Jack Bull.

JACK BULL
He told me to run, Jake. He told me –

JAKE
Did you see who they are?

JACK BULL
Jayhawkers, Jake. Lawrence men –

They both crouch as they hear the sounds of riders coming towards them.

JAKE
C'mon!

Jake grabs his friend and moves him into the darkness of the woods.

We hear their hurried footsteps as they move off into the night, the sound of fire and screaming behind them.

EXT. STOREHOUSE/CROSSROADS – DAY

A dusty crossroads. It's one year later. A couple of Union Scouts lounge warily in front of a storehouse as a middle-aged man helps a couple of other troops load up a wagon with supplies. One of the Scouts takes a swig from a jug and hands it to the other. He elbows his comrade, noticing a small group of Riders approaching. The Scouts rise.

Three other Union Soldiers ride up, accompanied by a horse, over which is slung the body of Jake Roedel. Blood congeals on the back of his filthy hemp shirt; his lifeless arms dangle toward the ground. He's bearded, smudged, vacant-eyed.

> RIDER #1
>
> Gentlemen. Captain Henderson, Company D.

A casual salute. Two of the Riders unhitch Jake's body and let it slump to the ground with a thump.

> FEDERAL SCOUT #1
>
> You boys have rid a bit far from home.

The Riders dismount.

> RIDER #1
>
> Spent two nights tracking this bushwhacking bastard and his Confederate friends through the Sni-a-bar. What are you boys doin' this far into Missouri?

> FEDERAL SCOUT #1
>
> Just rootin' out secesh and conscriptin' chickens. We been through all of Cass and Lafayette counties – killed our share.

14 INT. STOREHOUSE – DAY

The group enters the building – more of a shack than a store. The Shopkeeper sets up drinks on a makeshift counter. As the three Riders place themselves in the room, we begin to notice details about their uniforms – mismatched boots, missing buttons, etc. As the first Rider raises a glass, we notice the side of his uniform is riddled with bullet holes. The blood around them is barely noticeable in the dark.

FEDERAL SCOUT #2

Not much action in Lafayette. But we got four of 'em Sunday
last.

FEDERAL SCOUT #1

Stretched their necks.

FEDERAL SCOUT #2

They're still hanging –

FEDERAL SCOUT #1

New orders – we're s'posed to kill any Southern types who
might want to cut 'em down and give them a proper burial.
(*to Scout #2*)
Hey, George, fetch that busthead out there.

RIDER #1

So you men were in on Lafayette?

FEDERAL SCOUT #1

Yes sir. But we're tirin' of chasin' these guerrillas into the
bush. You can't trust none of these locals – they're all hidin'
'em. I wish we had a real army to fight, not these sneakin'
bastards.

RIDER #2 (PITT)

Battles and armies – all that's back East. Here in Missouri,
you just have the people to fight you.

15 EXT. STOREHOUSE – DAY

*The other Scout walks back outside, and stares for a moment at the
horses. He frowns. The body is missing.*

FEDERAL SCOUT #2

Hey, Ted! Ted?!

*He spins around to face the 'dead' bushwhacker, now very much alive,
holding a pistol to his face.*

JAKE ROEDEL

So, you boys were in on Lafayette, eh?

He shoots him square in the face.

Inside, the other three riders swiftly and calmly draw their pistols and gun down the other soldiers.

Silence, as Jake walks into the store.

The Storekeeper and his wife huddle against the counter.

The Riders take off their Union caps and shake out their long bushwhacker hair. Among them is Jack Bull, older and tougher-looking. They remove the rest of their Federal uniforms to reveal hemp and flannel shirts; pistols are tucked in belts, pockets, everywhere.

> RIDER #1 (BLACK JOHN AMBROSE)
> Doin' business with the Yankee invaders?

> STOREKEEPER
> Now, they forced me –

Pitt Mackeson shoots the shopkeeper, puts his gun back. The Woman runs to her fallen husband. She looks up tearfully to Black John.

> STOREKEEPER'S WIFE
> He's dead. You killed him. Shoot me too, please.

> BLACK JOHN
> *(stepping over her to check the contents of the cash drawer)*
> We don't hurt women.

Pitt lights a match and starts a fire when Jake walks over and snuffs it out.

> JAKE
> We took her man. Leave her the store.

Pitt just looks at Jake, lights another match, and sets a bundle of linens on fire. Jake is about to respond when Jack Bull steps up and comes between them.

> JACK BULL
> C'mon, Jake, it's gettin' hot in here.

> BLACK JOHN
> Enough of this, boys. Let's load up.

17 EXT. STOREHOUSE – DAY

Smoke pours from the storehouse. The Woman has managed to pull the body of her husband from the store.

The boys have hitched up the wagon full of supplies. They ride off.

18 EXT. RIVERSIDE – DAY

The boys ride along.

19 EXT. BUSHWHACKER ENCAMPMENT – DAY

The boys stop by a picket.

The gang rides into a makeshift encampment in the woods. There are about fifteen other men already in the camp. George Clyde (handsome, Scottish but raised in the South) greets Black John as the men dismount.

> BLACK JOHN
>
> George Clyde!

> GEORGE CLYDE
>
> Black John, Pitt. Well met, my men, well met!

> PITT MACKESON
>
> What news have you?

> GEORGE CLYDE
>
> News? None of that, but I do have a question, and one of great import and urgency, for all of you men, the answer to which will be recompensed with a bootful of whiskey.

> PITT MACKESON
>
> And what would this question be?

> GEORGE CLYDE
>
> Well . . .
>
> (*thinking*)
>
> If a six-teated she-dog runs ten miles an hour shittin' splinters, how swift need she be to shit a rockin' chair?

> PITT MACKESON
>
> Well, if she ate a possum belly she could shit the chair whole if she was swimmin'!

The men laugh. Jake and Jack Bull wander on.

20 EXT. BUSHWHACKER ENCAMPMENT – DAY

Jake and Jack Bull throw their bedding down and wander over to where Cave Wyatt is playing cards with young Riley Crawford.

>   RILEY
> I got all puppies' feet – do I win the money?

>   CAVE WYATT
> Puppies' feet! Can you fathom that? Puppies' feet. Them's
> clubs, you damned child.
>   (*throws his cards on the blanket, scooping up the money*)
> No more gamblin' – I can't enjoy it like his.

Riley takes a childish affront.

>   RILEY
> Just who you think you're damning, Cave?

>   CAVE WYATT
>   (*menacing*)
> Did I hurt your feelings, son?

>   RILEY
>   (*childish again*)
> Well, it was rude of you.

>   CAVE WYATT
> Well, I do apologize. And here – you can even have back
> some of the winnings I just stole from you.

Everyone laughs.

21 EXT. BUSHWHACKER ENCAMPMENT – DAY

Later, Cave Wyatt passes a jug to Jack Bull, who sits besides Jake.

>   CAVE WYATT
> You boys'll love ridin' with George Clyde. He makes Yankee-
> killin' as entertaining a pastime as greasin' ganders.

Across the encampment from them sits a large, brooding black man. He has an array of pistols spread out in front of him, and is methodically cleaning them.

> JAKE
>
> Whose guns are those?

> CAVE WYATT
>
> You mean Holt over there? Oh, you'll get used to him – that's George Clyde's pet nigger, but don't call him that in front of George. No, George don't like that.

> JAKE
>
> He carries those?

> CAVE WYATT
>
> He's a damned fine scout, and spy – and, when George tosses him a gun, a good Yankee-killer too. You know Clyde and him growed up together, and when Jim Lane's boys came for Clyde, Holt there sent three of 'em to heaven – so now he rides with us, 'cause them Yankees want to kill him real bad.

> JAKE
>
> Yeah? Well, a nigger with guns – it still is a nervous thing to me.

Cave laughs and hands him a jug.

Holt eyes the men deliberately, as he lines the guns up in front of him with methodical precision. George Clyde sits down silently beside him, and joins him in his work.

22 EXT. SKY – DUSK

The light falls.

23 EXT. ENCAMPMENT – NIGHT

Jack Bull and Jake bunk down together.

> JAKE
>
> Jack Bull?

> JACK BULL
>
> Yes, Jake.

JAKE

Well, I been watching these stars now for a long time.

JACK BULL

Uh-huh.

JAKE

Every night, for nigh on a year.

JACK BULL

Uh-huh.

JAKE

And you've heard tell, the stars are supposed to have some
sway on our doings down here below?

JACK BULL

I've heard it said from time to time, but where are you going,
Jake, with all this philosophy, because I am just about ready
to shoot you if you don't let me get on to my sleeping.

JAKE

Well, Jack Bull, I was about to utter a profound sentence on
the relation between those stars and our precious assholes,
but you done made me forget the thought of it.

JACK BULL

Then go to sleep, Roedel. And keep from thinking.
Dutchmen think too much. It's bothersome.

24 EXT. CLARK FARM — DAY

*Mrs Clark, a sympathizer, cautiously comes out on to the porch. Her
twelve-year-old teenage daughter looks out from the window.*

Black John and Pitt Mackeson ride up; the others hold back.

PITT MACKESON

We're looking for the Dorris place.

MRS CLARK

It's just up the road. Who are you?

BLACK JOHN

Why, we are Southern men. And hungry.

MRS CLARK

You don't look like Southern men. How do I know?

Riley Crawford comes forward.

RILEY CRAWFORD

Woman, my name is Crawford. One of the Six-Point Creek
Crawfords – do you know me?

MRS CLARK

I knew the father. Come on and eat as what we have.

*Riley and Black John tie their horses to the front porch, as the others
lead theirs behind the barn.*

25 INT. CLARK HOUSE – DAY

*As the men enter the house, Jake approaches Mrs Clark as she and her
daughter work in the kitchen.*

JAKE

You alone here?

MRS CLARK

Yes . . . well, no. My man is at Arkansas with Shelby. My son
is in the barn.

JAKE

Is he grown?

MRS CLARK

He was. He gave up a leg at Wilson's Creek. I keep him hid
away. Union Jayhawkers would kill him.

JAKE

He should come with us.

MRS CLARK

No. He won't fight. He's done with that.

Jake walks into the parlor, and taps Jack Bull on the shoulder.

JACK BULL

Where?

                              JAKE
    The barn.

26 EXT. CLARK HOUSE – DAY

Jack Bull and Jake walk cautiously towards the barn.

27 INT. CLARK BARN – DAY

*Light streams into the half-burnt barn, turning the space into a mixture
of dark recesses and glaring pools of light. The boys squint, hearing a
low snicker from the other side of the barn.*

                          JACK BULL
    Halloo inside. We are friends, Clark. Show yourself.

*The sniggering increases in volume. The boys see that it comes from a
hay pile behind a fallen rafter. A small man lays there, a shotgun by his
side.*

                           CLARK
    Bushwhackers. I could've killed you both – but it ain't even
    loaded.

                            JAKE
    No need of that. We're friends.

                           CLARK
    You s'pose so, do you? I don't.

                            JAKE
    You were at Wilson's Creek. Who with?

                           CLARK
    Why, with General Price. The fat glory-hound rebel himself.

*Jack Bull crouches besides Clark, and points at the stump which is all
that remains of one of Clark's legs.*

                          JACK BULL
    Didn't see that one comin', eh?

                           CLARK
                       (laughing again)
    I saw it comin'. I saw it rollin' past little piles of meat and

                             19

bone that I once called my friends. I watched it roll right up to me.

JACK BULL

If you saw it comin', couldn't you have dodged it?

CLARK

Well, nature borned me smart, and that changes things – I wanted my foot broke so I could head home, and that damned little cannon ball was goin' slower'n a fevered rabbit –

JAKE

Why you are a fool, a cannon ball will rip your leg –

Clark just resumes his laugh.

JACK BULL

Well, General Price is a good man. Would you have us fetch you something to eat?

CLARK

I have a mother for that. I don't eat anyway. I'm tryin' somethin' different.

JAKE

You'll be killed anyways. Jayhawkers or militia, someone or the other will stop here and kill you.

CLARK

Aw, they been here already and burned the barn. I wouldn't even move to put it out. Ma done it. As likely you boys will kill me. I don't much care.

JACK BULL

You want to die. Perhaps you would choose to die now.

He pulls his pistol and aims it at Clark's head.

I've some experience in the killing line, Clark. I could do you a fair job of it, this minute.

Clark ponders.

CLARK

No. No. Ma has her heart set on me livin'.

JACK BULL

You sure of that? I'm here and now loaded.

CLARK

I don't believe so.

Jack Bull slowly holsters his pistol and walks to the door.

JACK BULL

Your mother is a fine enough woman. You might help her
some, don't you think? You get yourself a stick to lean on and
walk around a bit.

CLARK

Uh-huh. That could be next. That could be the very next
thing.

Jake and Jack Bull exit.

28 INT. CLARK FARM – DAY

*Jake is sitting, eating with Jack Bull. Across the room, Pitt Mackeson
and Cave Wyatt eat, their eyes on Jake. Pitt takes out his bowie knife
and carves into his ham.*

CAVE WYATT

You're an interestin' foreigner, Jake.

JAKE

Why is that?

CAVE WYATT

I hear your pa's a Deutschman, but you are loyal to here and
not the North. Uncommon.

JACK BULL

Jake may have been born a Deutschman, but my ma and pa
practically raised him – he's as Southern as they come.

Jake, pretending indifference, yawns and picks up his plate.

He walks alone out on to the front porch.

29 EXT. CLARK FARM – DAY

Jake lies down on the porch to take a nap.

A light breeze drifts through the trees. He closes his eyes.

Almost inaudibly, he hears a faint click – he opens his eyes, staring down the barrel of a Federal soldier's carbine. The Federal stands next to another soldier, and there are fifteen more of them fanning out from the road in the background, encircling the house.

> FEDERAL #1
> (*nodding to the two horses*)
> Where's the other one, you devil? Speak up and maybe you'll live yet.

A few of the other Federals laugh at this.

> JAKE
> I am alone. That's my daddy's horse – he was shot off it three days back.

> FEDERAL #2
> He lies. Let's parole him to Jesus, and right now.

At that moment, gunfire blasts from the windows inside the house. Two of the Federals fall. Jake races across the porch.

> JACK BULL
> (*from inside*)
> Get in here, Jake!

> JAKE
> Let me get the horses!

As Jake runs out to grab the horses, the militia lets loose another volley. The horses are hit, and Jake hightails it around and back to the house.

As he runs back, the bullets whiz by him. One of them clefts his pinkie finger on his left hand. It lands in the chicken pen near the porch.

30 INT. CLARK HOUSE – DAY

> JAKE
> (*bursting into the door*)
> Damn! They took my pinkie!

The shooting continues.

Jake wraps a kerchief around his severed finger.

Damn!

BLACK JOHN

Don't fret about that now.

The Bushwhackers are arrayed at every window and corner, trading voluminous fire with the militia. Splinters, bullets, glass fly everywhere.

BLACK JOHN
(*shouting out of the window*)
Do you kill women? There's women in here!

The shooting stops.

SOLDIER
(*from outside*)
You know we don't kill women! Send them out now and they'll be safe-passaged!

Turner Rawls turns to the Woman.

TURNER RAWLS
Please, ma'am, you and your daughter got to go.

MRS CLARK
We're goin', son. You best believe it. There ain't no way we're not goin'!

She takes her daughter's arm in hers and walks, dignified but quickly, out of the house and up towards the barn.

TURNER
We can't hold them from here.

BLACK JOHN
Stand fast, boys. We'll kill them yet.

31 EXT. CLARK HOUSE – DAY

Just as he speaks, several men, under a ferocious covering fire, push a wagon filled with burning hay up to the house, tossing torches at the roof.

23

Smoke starts to pour into the house.

CAVE WYATT
We'll just have to take our chances runnin'!

BABE HUDSPETH
They'll riddle us down! Shit, there ain't so much as a stump out there for cover.

Two of the youngest Bushwhackers, Starke Helms and Lawson, crawl under a bed in the side parlor.

Black John kicks the bed.

BLACK JOHN
Come on, men, let's go to it.

Standing by the back door are George Clyde and Holt. Clyde hands Holt one of his pistols, who checks it quickly and carefully. Then, nodding silently to each other, they burst out of the door –

Running sideways, back to back, firing methodically, like a precision machine, the two are entirely in sync.

After a moment of stunned awe, Jake, Jack Bull and the rest of the men barrel out after them.

It's a chicken shoot. Turner is shot through the cheek but makes it to his horse.

Others are killed as they exit the house.

George Clyde and Holt are the only ones doing consistent damage, as, following them, Pitt Mackeson, Black John, Jake, Jack Bull, Riley Crawford, Cave Wyatt and a couple of others make it into the woods behind the house and mount their horses as the bullets fly.

32 EXT. WOODS – DAY

A horse chase and fire fight ensue in the woods.

In close quarters, the Federals pursue the Bushwhackers.

Men are knocked from their horses in the thick tangle of branches and woods.

A Federal Soldier takes aim at Jake, whose horse is ensnared in some brush. As he is about to fire, Holt rides by him and shoots him off his mount.

A Bushwhacker circles behind the Federal Militiamen and fires, close range, behind them, before being shot down.

Jake and Jack Bull carry on a running battle until they break across a cow path and into a stand of scrub oak and dry stumps.

Screams and ad libs throughout.

> **FIGHTERS**
> (*ad lib*)
> I got one! Down there, boy! This way, men!

In the midst of the action, we hear Black John shouting orders.

> **BLACK JOHN**
> Split up! We'll meet at The Place!

Throughout the gunfight, the Bushwhackers' extraordinary horsemanship and quick-shooting are evident.

33 EXT. WOODS – DAY

Jake, Jack Bull, George Clyde, Holt and Turner Rawls, his face shot through, slowly ride through the brush, taking stock.

Babe Hudspeth rides up.

> **BABE HUDSPETH**
> Where's my brother? Did you see my brother?

Turner Rawls speaks with difficulty, his mouth still filled with blood.

> **TURNER RAWLS**
> Bock yawn. Woof him. Alibe.

> **BABE HUDSPETH**
> With Black John? Alive?

Turner nods yes.

> **JACK BULL**
> That was sure enough hot. I think I killed one. They left us hurting – that's certain.

They ride on.

34 EXT. PATH – DAY

The sky darkens above them as they ride.

35 EXT. PATH – EVENING

Later. A cold drizzle now falls on them.

36 EXT. HOG PATH – EVENING

The rain continues as the men straggle along.

They come to a crossroads. Babe Hudspeth stops.

> BABE HUDSPETH
> I believe, if I ain't lost, that one mile over there we'll find Mr
> Daily's house. I've stopped there before. He's a Southern
> man.

> JAKE
> Let's make a visit.

*Jake is about to ride on to the road, when Holt bolts his horse forward
and grabs the reins of Jake's horse, pulling it back.*

> What in almighty – ?

*Holt slips off his horse and in an instant has unrolled his blanket on the
roadway. George Clyde dismounts and hands Holt another blanket,
which he lays beside the first one. Holt leads his horse carefully over the
blankets across the road.*

> GEORGE CLYDE
> (*to Jake*)
> That's how you cover your tracks, children.
> (*beat*)
> Holt here may not gab much, but he'll teach you boys more
> than a thing or two 'bout bushwackin'.

Jack Bull raises his eyebrows at Jake.

37 EXT. DAILY HOUSE – DUSK

Establishing shot: a modest farmhouse.

38 INT. DAILY HOUSE – NIGHT

*The men are gathered in the simple parlor, as Mrs Daily clears food –
squirrel and biscuits with thin pan gravy – and shoos away her two
small children. Holt sits silently in a corner.*

>   MR DAILY
> There's more of 'em every day. I'm surprised you boys
> haven't headed further south, what with the numbers of
> Federals pouring in from Lawrence.

>   GEORGE CYLDE
> We still get some work done.

>   MR DAILY
> I heard Sweet Springs was shot up some.

>   JACK BULL
> We were in on that.

>   MR DAILY
> I was told you killed Schmidt and Ogilvy – is it so?

>   JACK BULL
>   (*shrugging*)
> Did we? I know we killed some of 'em. I know that.

>   JAKE
> Schmidt was one. He was the runner.

39 INT. DAILY HOUSE – NIGHT

*A half-hour later, the men, drinking from a big jug, are already a bit
drunk and giggly.*

>   MR DAILY
> I been to New Orleans once. And there I met upon a woman.
> Well, she had shaved herself complete. There wasn't a hair
> left on her. She was just like a peeled apple.

BABE HUDSPETH

This is disgusting. But why would she do it?

JACK BULL

Why, to set one whore apart from another. Showmanship.

MR DAILY

It is a damned fine show, too. I could see it again and still be interested.

They laugh. Mrs Daily enters.

MRS DAILY

Mr Daily, I will not have you getting drunk in my home.

MR DAILY

I am not drunk. I am entertaining our company.

MRS DAILY

You are drunk, Claude. It is ever so plain to me that you are drunk.

MR DAILY

Nah, I'm not drunk, Sal. I'm barely happy – could a drunk man do this?

Daily begins a jig around the jug, which sits on the bare plank floor in front of him.

He dances expertly, kicking ever closer to the jug, but never touching it. The whole house rocks in steady cadence with his kicks. The men clap in time for him.

Flushed and finished, he ends the jig with a tight whirl.

Does that prove it? I never nudged it.

MRS DAILY

You shame me. Only a drunk man would dance around that way.

She turns and walks out.

MR DAILY

Aw!

He stumbles out after her.

Jake whispers to Jack Bull.

> JAKE
> How can a man put up with it?

> JACK BULL
> That is a question neither of us is likely to answer.

40 EXT. MCCORKLE'S ENCAMPMENT – DAY

The gang enters the encampment. There are more men here than at the earlier camp.

Black John comes up.

> BLACK JOHN
> Good day, boys. You see the present that Coleman brought us? Four Federals – he took 'em from the Kansas City mail train.

They look over at the four prisoners, linked together by a thick rope, anchored to a tree.

Several of Coleman's group sit on the ground watching the prisoners, taunting them.

Holt silently plants himself nearby, though at a discreet distance.

> RILEY

Are those good boots, Yank?

> PRISONER #1

I don't know. Could be.

> RILEY

They seem to run a mite slow.

> PRISONER #1

This time they did.

> RILEY

Well, there won't be any more races for them with you standin' in them, will there?

> PRISONER #1

I would reckon not.

Jake has walked over to the group.

From off-screen we hear a voice.

> ALF BOWDEN

Jake, oh my, Jake.

Jake turns to discover his old neighbour tied up with the other prisoners. (We have glimpsed Alf Bowden briefly at the wedding.)

> JAKE

Hello, Alf. You sure are in a fix.

> ALF BOWEN

It seems so. It surely does seem so.

Pitt Mackeson walks by.

> PITT MACKESON

You know this man?

JAKE

Certainly. His daddy's place is just downriver from the Chileses'. Hemp growers.

Jack Bull comes up.

ALF

Jack Bull.

JACK BULL

Alf Bowden. Any news of home?

ALF BOWDEN

No, no, no. It all just goes on. Some may have died, not most.

JACK BULL

What of my mother?

ALF BOWDEN

Well, now, well. She is watched. All the secesh are watched.

JAKE

And my father?

ALF BOWDEN

He comes and goes – he's a Union man – he ain't bothered by no one. But, you know this, you must know the whole town talks of you out here black flaggin' it. Some friendliness may be lost for your kin.

JACK BULL

Have you been fed?

ALF BOWDEN

Not so's you'd notice.

JACK BULL

I'll look into it.

Jack Bull walks off, as a voice is heard behind them.

BLACK JOHN

Roedel!

Jake is set up at a makeshift writing stand with paper and pen. George Clyde, Pitt Mackeson and Black John stand round him.

BLACK JOHN

Now take this down. It is for the *Lexington Union News*, so do it fine, the way you do.

JAKE

Gladly.

BLACK JOHN

Dear Citizens, Mistakes are most common these days and deadly for it. The Federals are to hang William Lloyd and James Curtin, two fine sons of Missouri. By a provident cut of the cards four Federals have been dealt to me. It is their hope that Lloyd and Curtin are not hanged, as they would provide the sequel to such murders. But if our men are released, I will, as a gentleman, release the unfortunates. The choice is yours, citizens. Make it wisely.

PITT MACKESON

Wait a minute. You need to tell the citizens we'll come and kill *them*, too.

BLACK JOHN

Oh, they *know* that.
> (*beat*)
Now add, Signed John Ambrose and George Clyde, Commanding, First Kansas Irregulars.

CLYDE

That's good. And put a note on it that says: 'Where you think we ain't we are. Remember it!'

Jake finishes writing the letter.

JAKE

Who will deliver it? There are Federals all over Lexington.

PITT MACKESON

We can slip a man in there. We have done it before.

BLACK JOHN

Oh, I reckon a citizen could be pressed into service. If one can be found.

JAKE

That might be a job, for citizens are cautious hereabouts.

PITT MACKESON

You got some better idea, Dutchy? Maybe you would volunteer yourself, eh?

JAKE
(*thinking*)
There is a way to prove more things than one.
(*pointing to the prisoners*)
If we send a prisoner, it will prove we have prisoners and also he can attest to our intentions. It seems to me he could get more quickly into town as well, and time is short – Curtin and Lloyd will be hanged right quick, I would think.

Black John hums a tune for a bit while the others wait.

BLACK JOHN

It is a good idea. There are some fine touches to it.
(*patting Jake's shoulder*)
You should speak up more, Roedel, for you're not near so dumb as you let on.

JAKE

Aw.

BLACK JOHN

Now go put one of them Federals on a horse with that letter.

Pitt Mackeson eyes Jake warily as he walks to the prisoners.

43 EXT. MCCORKLE'S ENCAMPMENT – DAY

Jake walks briskly up to the prisoners – he kicks Alf Bowden with a measure of fake roughness.

JAKE

Get up you. You got travel ahead of you.

He gestures to the Bushwacker guarding the men to untie Alf Bowden.

As Jake leads Alf Bowden to a horse, we see him explaining what's happening.

JAKE

You are spared, Alf. But convince them to see this exchange through – it's only fair. We're only asking to be treated like the soldiers that we are, and we shall do your companions here the same courtesy.

Astride the horse, Alf looks down at Jake without saying anything, as Jake hands him the letter.

Do your best.

Alf kicks his horse and heads off without a word. Feeling someone standing behind him, Jake turns around to face Pitt Mackeson.

PITT MACKESON

I am on to you, Roedel.

JAKE

Don't get too much on to me, or I'll throw you off.

Pitt Mackeson simply smiles, then turns and goes.

Jake notices that Holt has been watching the encounter. Holt placidly looks at Jake.

And what are *you* lookin' at?

44 EXT. ENCAMPMENT – NIGHT

Jake and Jack Bull are lying in their bedrolls, under the stars. Jake is restless, staring up into the sky.

Jack Bull turns over and looks at him.

JACK BULL

What is it, Jake? I hear you ruminating louder than a cow chewing in my ear, and it is keeping me from my sleep.

JAKE

You think Alf Bowden's made it back to Lexington as yet? There was a minute there when I saw him riding off, I thought maybe you and me could join him, that we could all ride home together. Just ride back home.

JACK BULL

And what have you left at home that you're so anxious to ride back to?

JAKE

Nothing. Just a passel of memories. Mostly memories, of you and me, of your father, old Asa Chiles . . .

Jake sees that Jack Bull looks despondent at the mention of his father.

We'll stick together, Jack Bull. We'll get all of it back.

JACK BULL

Hah! And you are a black magician who can raise the dead, are you? No. My father is under the dirt to stay – like that –
(*pointing at Jake's nubbined left hand*)
– is gone to stay, too.

Jake holds up his hand.

JAKE

My finger? So it is. And it makes me notable by the loss.

JACK BULL

You sound pleased, as if that finger had been pestering you for rings.

JAKE

No, it was a fine finger. And I'd rather have it still, but it was took from me. It has been ate by chickens for sure. So I say, what is the good side to this amputation? And there is one.

JACK BULL

Name it, Jake.

JAKE

Well, say one day some Federals catch up to me and kill me in a thicket. And they would riddle me and hang me and no Southern man would find me for weeks or months, and when they did I'd be bad meat, pretty well rotted to a glob.

36

JACK BULL

That is scientifically accurate. I'm afraid I've seen it.

JAKE

I would be a glob of mysterious rot, and people would ask,
Who was that? And surely someone would look up and say,
Why it's nubbin-fingered Jake Roedel. Then you could go
and tell my father I was clearly murdered and he wouldn't be
tortured by uncertain wonders.

JACK BULL

And that's the good of it?

JAKE

Yessir. That's the good.

JACK BULL
(*incredulous*)

Go to sleep, Jake.

He rolls back over and closes his eyes.

45 EXT. WOODS NEAR MCCORKLE'S ENCAMPMENT – MORNING

*As Jake pees against a tree, he hears moans and screams coming from
the camp.*

46 EXT. MCCORKLE'S ENCAMPMENT – MORNING

From afar, Jake sees Black John pacing and ranting.

BLACK JOHN

Dead! Dead! Ripped to fragments! Oh yes, they have went
and done it to us! Treated them like pigs – worse than pigs!
Have at them boys – they shall be mementoes of our
resolve!

*Up near the tree, a small group, including Pitt Mackeson, is busy
torturing the Federal Prisoners. We don't see the details, but we can well
imagine the scene.*

CAVE WYATT
(*to Jake*)

They hanged and quartered Lloyd and Curtain last night. It

37

seems us Bushwhackers are not real soldiers. Not fit for trading, anyhow.

Jack Bull joins Jake as Cave walks away. They look up at the scene apprehensively.

> JACK BULL
> Say Jake, what are you knowing?

> JAKE
> I feel I am knowing too much.

> JACK BULL
> Aw well, forget it. Throw it down.

> JAKE
> We could of merely shot them.

> JACK BULL
> Well, Jake, that was not the plan. There may be no rhyme to it, but that was just plain old not the plan.

Jake nods.

47 EXT. MCCORKLE'S ENCAMPMENT – NIGHT

Jake and Jack Bull sit and clean their pistols by the firelight. George Clyde, Cave Wyatt, Riley Crawford, Holt, Pitt Mackeson and a few other men come up.

Cave throws a small sack down in front of Jake.

> CAVE
> Black John says you're lettered. It's Union mail. He wants you to look it over and tell him if there's anything to learn.

Jake spills the contents of the sack out on to the ground.

> JAKE
> (*looking through*)
> Aw. It's just stuff from up north – there's no military intelligence in here.

The men sit down around the small pile.

CAVE
Yeah? Well, maybe you could read it to us just the same.

Pitt takes one from the pile.

PITT
Yeah, read us this letter, Dutchy.

JAKE
It's someone else's letter.

PITT
Was. I want to hear you read it.

JAKE
I don't think I care to.

PITT
Oh, is that so? I think if you think a little more, Dutchy, that you'll think you *do* want to read me it. Right now, too.

RILEY
Yes. How do you know but there might be secrets in it? Read it at us.

Jake senses trouble and relents.

JAKE

All right.

(*taking the letter*)

This here is from Mrs Mary Williams, of Bear Lake Wisconsin. 'Dear Sons, No word of you in so long. Right past first frost of the year last. Your father is better, but his feet are still bloated and he won't walk right on them.'

The men shift around.

CAVE

That's thicked-up blood does that. Thicked-up blood bloats the feet.

JAKE

Uh-huh. 'A fire hit the old church. Burned down. The new one was just ready so no great trouble was had of it. Margaret has married since the frost of this year last. You wouldn't know it, for how could you? Her husband is Walter Maddox. He is out of the war, with one arm busted at New Madrid but it works fine enough. The dirt was turned over and the smell and deepness gave me heart. It is just black-rich. You boys know how that is.'

RILEY

My daddy was up there. He was up there way before they hung him. He said the dirt was so rich you could ate it like porridge.

JACK BULL

They have very good dirt up there, but a short grow season.

CAVE

It sounds like *real* good dirt to me.

JAKE

'That girl Dave got sweet for is in town and still single and about. She asks of you but I have no news since first frost of the year last. Without news I cannot answer her. You are both missed here. Your Mother.'

The men are lulled to a temporary silence.

> **RILEY**
> She sounds about like my mother, that old woman does.

> **JACK BULL**
> One mother is much like another.

> **CAVE**
> But remember one thing. Her boys will kill you if they can.

Jake folds up the letter, then tosses it into the fire.

48 EXT. MCCORKLE'S ENCAMPMENT/WOODS – DAY

Autumn colors fade as dying and dead leaves swirl in the breeze.

49 EXT. MCCORKLE'S ENCAMPMENT – DAY

Autumn. Some of the men are circled around Black John.

> **BLACK JOHN**
> It is time for our winter hibernation. I have gathered the
> names of loyal Southerners who shall provide for us. We'll
> group in fours – and I'll send word the beginning of spring for
> where to rendezvous. I need not rehearse to you all the
> dangers of unnecessary movement during the coming winter
> months.

*Babe Hudspeth and John Nolan, a black spy working for the
bushwhackers, enter the camp.*

*They speak with Black John in the background as the men pack up the
camp.*

*Babe Hudspeth walks towards Jake and Jack Bull, who loiter near
their horses with Holt and George Clyde. George Clyde consults a piece
of paper.*

> **GEORGE CLYDE**
> We shall to the Evans farm, boys. Their place is but half a
> mile from the Willards, where there resides a certain Miss
> Juanita to whom, if I do not flatter myself, my attentions are
> not unfavorably regarded.

JAKE

You mean we are to spend the winter in Lafayette solely on
account that you are sweet on Juanita Willard?

GEORGE CLYDE

As good a reason as any, Dutchy.

Babe Hudspeth reaches them.

He shakes hands, then sits. They sit with him.

BABE HUDSPETH

Nolan's brought some news from home. Hank Pattison is
murdered. Our old neighbor Jantzen got him with his gang of
militia.

JACK BULL

That is sad. He was a good Southern man. What of Thomas
Pattison?

BABE HUDSPETH

Oh, he is murdered, too. And Sally Burgess married a
Federal from Michigan. Her whole family hides their faces.
(*pause*)
And, well, Dutchy, that Federal Alf Bowden – he rode
straight from here and killed your father.

Babe pulls off his hat and holds it in his hands.

He shot him in the neck down by the river, then booted him
along Main Street 'til he died.

JAKE

I spared Alf Bowden. You all know it.

JACK BULL

You taught him mercy, but he forgot the lesson.

Jack Bull puts a hand on Jake's shoulder.

(*beat*)

JAKE

My father. My father was a Unionist. Like all the Germans.
An Unconditional Unionist.

42

Well, yeah, but he was mainly known as your father, Dutchy.
You got a reputation now.

Jake walks away.

50 EXT. WOODS NEAR MCCORKLE ENCAMPMENT – DAY

Jack Bull walks to where Jake sits and joins him.

JACK BULL
Hey there, Dutchy.

JAKE
You let the rest of 'em call me that, but you, you call me by
my name.

JACK BULL
Jacob.

They clasp hands and shake on it.

Jake looks off.

JAKE
You know, I never really thought of him as my father. Until I
killed him.

51 EXT. FOREST PATH – DAY

*Jake, Jack Bull, Holt and George Clyde ride the path. Jake looks up at
the wintry sun.*

52 EXT. EVANSES' HOUSE – DAY

*A desolate, winter landscape. The boys walk their horses back into the
woods.*

*Mr Evans comes out of the big, empty house, looking around nervously.
From behind a window, we see Mrs Evans, young Mary, their
daughter, and Sue Lee Shelley, the pretty nineteen-year-old who
married Mr Evans's son.*

*They watch the backs of men in silence as they walk their horses behind
the house.*

53 EXT. WOODS – DAY

In a clearing in the woods, the men tie up their horses.

Mr Evans walks up, a pickaxe and shovel in his hands.

> **MR EVANS**
> I'm sorry we can't offer you proper hospitality, but with the
> Federal patrols –

George Clyde takes the axe and shovel from him.

> **GEORGE CLYDE**
> We're much obliged. May I ask after Mrs Evans?

> **MR EVANS**
> My wife? She is as well as can be expected. Our other Mrs
> Evans, that's Sue Lee – well, she was a Mrs Evans for but
> three weeks, until my son joined our Confederate forces.
> *(pause)*
> He was killed in the fighting at Independence.

> **JACK BULL**
> We're sorry to hear of it.

> **MR EVANS**
> Yes. Well, you boys lay low here, and we'll come by from
> time to time with provisions such as there are.

54 EXT. DUGOUT – DAY

The shovel drives into the lightly frosted earth.

*Jack Bull throws up a mound of dirt, then hands off the shovel to
George Clyde. There is already quite a pit dug.*

Jake works the pickaxe, then hands it to Holt.

> **JACK BULL**
> It has been a while since we've done work. There is
> something soothing about it.

> **GEORGE CLYDE**
> *(laughing)*
> Work has never been my main ambition.

> (*putting his hand on Holt's shoulder*)
We have done much work, but I think I've spied an easier
way to riches.

JACK BULL

Spell out this miracle.

GEORGE CLYDE

Why, you just ride up and take it.

JACK BULL

Ah, it's the good old rule, the simple plan.

GEORGE CLYDE

It's a workable method – that is proven.

JAKE

I don't know that the time is yet right for robbin' wholesale.

GEORGE CLYDE

You don't know enough, then. It's as right as two rabbits.

55 EXT. DUGOUT – DAY

Jack Bull jumps into the pit – the dugout is much further along.

JACK BULL

Hmmm. We should face south – we all know that – but the
horses should be near the door.

GEORGE CLYDE

Whatever you think, Jack Bull. I just can't get enough of this
sweaty work, so you go on and figure it out right.

They all laugh.

56 INT. DUGOUT – DAY

*Holt and George Clyde roll in flat rocks to lay the chimney, as Jack
Bull oversees the work. The dugout is shaping up.*

JAKE
> (*from outside*)
Rider coming.

George Clyde grabs his guns.

GEORGE CLYDE
Aw, let's go see our visitor.

57 EXT. DUGOUT – DAY

They walk out and take positions around the dugout.

*As the horse comes into view, we see that the rider is wearing a dress.
It's Sue Lee.*

SUE LEE
It's just me. Don't shoot or some dumb thing like that.

Jack Bull, the natural aristocrat, sweeps his hat.

JACK BULL
Why, how do? You must be Mrs Evans.

SUE LEE
I've brung you some dinner. I'm – I'm glad to meet you Mr –

JACK BULL
Chiles, Jack Bull Chiles, and this here is Jake Roedel, and –

GEORGE CLYDE
George Clyde, Mrs Evans.

SUE LEE
Mr Evans wishes me to apologize for not having sent you feed
sooner. The Federals have been on the move. And don't you
call me Mrs Evans. My name is Sue Lee Shelley. It's a good
one and I'm a widow now, so I reckon I'll go back to it and
use it.

JACK BULL
Please pardon me. But won't you please come on in? It's not
much to gaze on, but I reckon we can essay some hospitality.

*George Clyde pulls open the plank used as a door over the dugout and
Sue Lee steps into the doorway.*

GEORGE CLYDE
After me, ma'am.

46

As she passes by him, George Clyde gives Jack Bull a series of winks and slinging elbows, as the two of them follow her in.

Jake stands, embarrassed, next to Holt.

> JAKE
> (*whispering, to himself*)

Damn.

Holt smiles.

What are you smilin' at?

> HOLT

I'll look to the horse.

Jake just stands there, completely stupefied.

> JAKE

Wait a second! What did you just say?

> HOLT

I said I'll see to the horse.

> JAKE

I know that! What I meant was how is it that you know how to talk?

> HOLT

Course I know how to talk. Now I'll look to the horse, Roedel. You'd best just get on in there and let the woman see your face.

> JAKE

Damnation, Holt, I believe I know best how to handle my personal affairs. Now – why don't you go see to the lady's horse, while I check on what she brung to eat.

58 INT. DUGOUT – DAY

Jake enters the dugout. Jack Bull gestures for him to take his hat off. He obliges.

> SUE LEE

My, aren't you Bushwhackers the gentlemen.

47

JACK BULL

We try to make the effort when possible. Do you think manners should be dropped in times like these?

59 INT. DUGOUT – DAY

Jake puts his hat back on his head.

SUE LEE

No. But I don't think horse sense ought to be dropped either. It's cold.

George Clyde and Jack Bull slap their hats back on their heads. Jake smiles slightly.

Sue Lee sits with her legs folded beneath her on a blanket on the floor.

JACK BULL

Hmm. You are so kind to think of us, ma'am.

SUE LEE

You men think of us more. You do the good work. I know it's dirty and dangerous.

GEORGE CLYDE

Those are good words to hear. It's not always we hear them.

SUE LEE
(*standing back up*)
Well now, I should be going. Mrs Evans will worry if I don't.

JACK BULL

We are awful sorry about Evans Junior, getting killed.

SUE LEE

We all suffer. But he suffers no more. He was a good husband to me. For three weeks he was a good husband, but he didn't last.

Holt enters.

What is *he* doing here, inside?

GEORGE CLYDE

Oh ma'am, this nigger's with me. His name is Holt.

SUE LEE
Perhaps he would be more useful off in a field, plowing.

GEORGE CLYDE
(*laughing*)
Oh, I would reckon not. No, ma'am. That's one nigger I wouldn't try to hitch behind a plow. Oh no, I wouldn't try that!

SUE LEE
Well, now. Oh yes, I almost forgot. Mr Evans asked that you come to the house tomorrow evening after dark. He is up on the Federal movements and could post you on them.

JACK BULL
Why, we'd be honored. Will you be joining us?

SUE LEE
Of course. There will be food.
(*laughing*)
I haven't yet trained myself to go without food.

JACK BULL
Look forward to it then.

She pauses before she leaves.

SUE LEE
(*nodding to Holt*)
I am not sure about him. Mr Evans –

GEORGE CLYDE
You've got nothing to worry about on that score.
(*barely suppressing his anger*)
You needn't worry about Holt. I'll be taking him with me over to the Willards tomorrow. We won't be coming to your dinner.

SUE LEE
Mr Clyde, honestly, I didn't mean to speak ill of your nigger.

GEORGE CLYDE
He's not *my* nigger. He's just a nigger who I trust with my life every day and night. That's all.

SUE LEE

That's very high praise.

GEORGE CLYDE

Yes, ma'am, it is.

SUE LEE

I see. Well, gentlemen, I really must take my leave. I hope the food will please you.

JAKE

It looks wonderful.

SUE LEE

Thank you. Now goodnight all.

Jack Bull jumps ahead of her to open the door-plank.

JAKE

Good night.

GEORGE CLYDE
(*sulking a bit*)

Night ma'am.

Jack Bull turns to Holt.

JACK BULL

Holt, the lady said goodnight to all. Touch your hat goodnight.

GEORGE CLYDE

Hey, Chiles, you don't tell him nothin'!

JACK BULL

He is being rude.

SUE LEE

Oh, gentlemen, please!

GEORGE CLYDE

He don't need tellin', Chiles!

HOLT

It's okay, George.
(*touching the brim of his hat with his fingers*)

50

'Night, missy.

> SUE LEE
> (*softly*)

Goodnight, Holt.

After she exits, Jack Bull pauses with a stare at George Clyde.

> JACK BULL

I will see her to her horse.

He closes the plank behind him.

> GEORGE CLYDE

Holt –

> HOLT

It weren't no hardship, George.

> JAKE
> (*picking up the grub bucket*)

Let's eat. Smells good.

> HOLT

It does. It surely does.

They spread out the food as Jack Bull re-enters the cabin. He sits down warily across from George Clyde.

No one speaks as they pass the food – bacon, corn-bread, potatoes.

Holt and Jake eat with relish as Clyde and Jack Bull pick at their food.

Jack Bull breaks the silence.

> JACK BULL

Holt, do you want my bacon?

Holt looks at him cautiously.

> HOLT

I could eat more.

> JACK BULL

Good.

He gets up and drops a meaty string on to Holt's plate.

HOLT

'Preciate it.

Clyde watches. They continue to eat in silence.

CLYDE

Roedel, you want *my* bacon?

JAKE

I guess I could eat it.

CLYDE
(*breaking into a smile*)
Well, I'll shit it behind the oak tree in the morning and you can just help yourself.

They all break into laughter.

60 EXT. EVANSES' HOUSE – NIGHT

Establishing shot.

61 INT. EVANSES' HOUSE PARLOR – NIGHT

Jack Bull, Jake and Mr Evans are gathered in the parlor for an after-dinner smoke and a drink of apple brandy. Jake is looking at the books on the shelves, and idly pulls one down.

MR EVANS

And why, if you do not mind my asking, did you not join the regular army?

JACK BULL

The army? Oh, we thought of it. But I suppose we decided this fight's got to be made in our own country, not where some general tells us it should happen.

MR EVANS
(*a pause*)
It will soon be everywhere. My family and I, we will be quitting this house in the spring. As soon as the roads are clear we will be trying for Texas.

JACK BULL

About half of Missouri has went to Texas.

MR EVANS

The whole state is thick with invaders. We cannot drive them away.

JACK BULL

We have different thoughts. I still want to fight. I reckon I will always want to fight them.

MR EVANS
(*almost to himself*)

Always . . .

There is an uncomfortable pause.

Have you ever been to Lawrence, Kansas, young man?

Jack Bull just lets loose a slight laugh.

JACK BULL

I reckon not, Mr Evans. I don't believe I'd be too welcome in Lawrence.

MR EVANS

No, I didn't think so. Before this war began my business took me there often. And as I saw those Northerners build that town, I witnessed the seeds of our destruction being sown.

JACK BULL

The founding of that town was truly the beginning of the Yankee invasion.

MR EVANS

I'm not speaking of numbers, nor even abolitionist trouble-making.
(*beat*)
It was the schoolhouse. Before they built a church even, they built that schoolhouse, and lettered every tailor's son and farmer's daughter in that country.

JACK BULL

Spelling won't help you hold a plow any firmer – or a gun either.

53

MR EVANS

No it won't, Mr Chiles. My point is merely – that they
rounded every pup up into that schoolhouse, because they
fancied that everyone should think and talk the same
freethinking way that they do, with no regard for station,
custom, or propriety. And that is why they will win – because
they believe everyone should live and think just like them.
And we shall lose because we don't care one way or the other
about how they live or think, we just worry about ourselves.

JACK BULL

Are you saying sir that we fight for nothing?

MR EVANS

Far from it, Mr Chiles. You fight for everything we ever had.
As did my son. It's just that we don't have it any more.

JACK BULL

Mr Evans, when you come back from Texas, it'll all be here
waiting for you. Jake and me, we'll see to it.

MR EVANS

Yes. Well, thank you, son. But enough of this war talk. Let's
have the ladies join us and think nobler thoughts.

JACK BULL

A fine idea. Some company would be splendid.

JAKE

Jack Bull, we should be thinking about getting on back.
Federals could pass by any time.

JACK BULL

Oh, put a gown on, Jake. It is too cold. They'll all be in front
of the fire examining their plunder.

Mrs Evans, Sue Lee and Mary, the girl, enter.

Sue Lee pours herself a brandy from the side table.

MRS EVANS

I have it in me to sing. Shall we have a sing-a-long?

MARY

Oh yes, I like those the best.

JACK BULL

My voice is not what it should be these days, but once it was
rumored I could carry a tune.

SUE LEE

And you, Mr Roedel?

JAKE

I believe I won't sing. Young ears are present.

SUE LEE

I'll bet you sing lovely.

JAKE

You would lose.

JACK BULL

He really does sing very poorly. He imitates the turkey first-
rate, though.

JAKE

I'd best do my gobblin' out of doors. You folks go ahead and
sing along, and I'll keep an eye on the roads.

MRS EVANS
(*along with other ad lib protestations*)

Do you really –

JACK BULL

Good man, Jake. I'll relieve you soon.

62 EXT. EVANS HOUSE – NIGHT

*Jake stands on the porch, looking up at the moon and at the moon-lit
road before him.*

*From inside, we hear the others singing – 'Barbry Allen', 'Kiss Me
Katie, Oh'.*

Jake shivers and rubs his hands together.

63 EXT. DUGOUT – DAY

Establishing shot.

64 INT. DUGOUT – DAY

Jake sits reading a book from Mr Evans' library.

Holt enters.

JAKE

Clyde back?

HOLT

I believe he's fixin' to spend a few more hours with Miss
Juanita. And Jack Bull?

JAKE

In the company of Mrs Sue Lee Evans.

HOLT

Sue Lee *Shelley.*

They both smile.

Jake?

JAKE

Yeah, Holt.

*Holt picks up a small sack from under his saddle bag, and walks with it
over to Jake.*

What's that?

*It's the mail sack taken earlier from the Federal prisoners. Jake takes it
and pours the letters out on to the floor.*

HOLT

I been keepin' 'em. No one learned me letters before, but
when you read them mails out loud it is something the likes I
never heard before. It made me think you could sometimes
try it again.

JAKE

So you packed those letters and kept 'em all this time?

Holt nods, a bit embarrassed.

> (*leaning down to pick up a few*)
> Well, these might not be too amusing. Might just be a bunch
> of boring thoughts from one stranger to another.

HOLT

The one you read from the mother was fine. I heard that one.
Do you recall it?

JAKE

Yes.

HOLT

She said things I enjoy to hear.

Jake holds a clutch of letters in his hand, and offers them to Holt.

JAKE

Okay, draw one.

Holt chooses one and Jake opens it.

> Okay, here goes. 'Dear Brother, I must write this right quick
> as I say goodbye to Massachusetts and our home in one hour.
> Yes, Danny, I have joined the fight, and a difficulter decision
> never before was made, as I've been just about the only
> eligible bachelor to dance with at Parlan's this past year. But
> without my favorite brother it is not the same, although the
> beer's been free as I've been drinking it with one of Parlan's
> daughters, which one I will not tell. Here's to you, Danny,
> and keep your head low out there. Bill.'

HOLT

It could get to where you might like that man.

JAKE

Yes. In other times he would not be so bad.

HOLT

But I liked the one from the mother best.

They pause to think on this.

JAKE

Holt, where is your mother?

HOLT

Aw, Kansas or Kingdom. I don't know. But I know she was
sold into Texas. I s'pose she is in Texas.

JAKE

How was that? Was it George that sold her?

Holt lets out a small, bitter laugh.

HOLT

No, sir. George and me, we growed up neighbors. It was
George that bought me out when Master Henry passed. But
he didn't have no means for ma or sister.

JAKE

So Clyde owns you?

HOLT

No, sir. Not in greenbacks and coppers, anyway. No, he don't
own me that way. He made of that a gift.

65 EXT. DUGOUT – DAY

A light snow falls as Sue Lee arrives.

66 INT. DUGOUT – DAY

*Holt tends to cleaning out the fireplaces. Jake and Jack Bull mend horse
gear.*

Sue Lee enters with two snowballs in her hands.

SUE LEE

Howdy!

*She hurls a snowball at Jake but misses and splatters Holt, who laughs
and throws the remnants on Jake. She walks over to Jack Bull and rubs
the other in his face.*

JAKE

You splattered poor Holt. Your aim is wild.

SUE LEE
It surely is!

She whirls around Jack Bull and shoves more snow down the back of his shirt.

JACK BULL
Whoa, mule! Settle down there.

Sue Lee pulls herself up.

SUE LEE
Mule? Whoa, mule?

JACK BULL
Uh, you just calm down.

She leans over him and pinches her cheeks.

SUE LEE
Do I look muley to you?

JACK BULL
Well, no.

She spins about, puts her hands on her knees, and sashays her butt practically into Jack Bull's nose.

SUE LEE
That look like a mule to you? That look like the rear end of an animal that heehaws in the night?

JACK BULL
It looks like it might could be.

Holt and Jake laugh.

SUE LEE
Jack Bull Chiles. Just because I'm a widow don't mean that you can get that familiar with me.

JACK BULL
Pardon me, ma'am, but I believe that it was you that shoved your rump into my face.

SUE LEE
Oh! That was only just to make a point.

JACK BULL
You made it. I will always know your rump from a mule's now. There are several differences. I don't know how I missed them before.

Sue Lee socks him on the chin.

He springs to his feet and grabs her, putting his arms around her.

SUE LEE
Now don't be mean. I can't tolerate meanness.

He pulls her face into his and they start to kiss.

Holt and Jake look away, hang dog.

After a spell, the kissing breaks off.

JACK BULL
Is that too mean?

SUE LEE
(*in a tiny voice*)
No, it's really not too mean at all.

She backs off and straightens herself out.

Oh goodness.

JACK BULL

Yes, goodness is what it is.

This breaks Jake's patience.

JAKE

Aw, for crying out loud! We're sitting right here. Show us some mercy.

Jack Bull shoots him a look.

SUE LEE

He is quite right. I better get to the house.

JAKE

And cover your tracks in the snow, too. You'll be leading curious Federals right on to us.

JACK BULL

Now don't be rude. You have no reason to be rude.

JAKE

Is that so? There happens to be a war going on everywhere but between your ears, you dumb ox.

Jack Bull quickly lands a kick square in Jake's chest.

JACK BULL

Dumb ox, am I?

Jake sits, struggling for breath.

I'm sorry, Jake. My leg just did that on its own. There was no thought behind it.

JAKE

I hear you. I hear you. But Holt and me ain't dyin' just so you can be kissed.

61

HOLT

Leave me out of this. I ain't even here. I ain't even nowhere near here.

Jack Bull laughs.

JACK BULL

I don't believe anyone is about to die from my kiss. In fact, she seems to be doing tolerably well.

SUE LEE

And well enough to get going, too. Good day.

She leaves.

After she's gone, Jack Bull points between his legs.

JACK BULL

Hey, looky here, boys.

JAKE

Where?

JACK BULL

Right here.

There's a big lump in his britches.

JAKE

My God, where's your shame, Chiles?

JACK BULL

Gone to Texas! Hoo-wee!

Jake doesn't look amused.

67 EXT. DUGOUT – DAY

We hear the muffled sounds of Jack Bull's whooping. The snow still falls gently, melting on the ground.

68 EXT. ROAD BY EVANSES' HOUSE – DAY

The road is frosted over. A column of Federal cavalry wends its way quietly down it.

From behind some trees, Holt and Jake watch. They trade glances, then head back into the forest.

69 EXT. DUGOUT – DAY

Jake and Jack Bull splitting firewood.

> JAKE
> You reckon George Clyde will ever join up with us again? Or do you think Juanita Willard will be his only cause and comfort from here on?

> JACK BULL
> Oh, George is efficient when it comes to comfort.

> JAKE
> This thing with Sue Lee and you, will it go on?

> JACK BULL
> I would reckon.

> JAKE
> Well, now, that is good for you.

> JACK BULL
> Yes, I believe I'll marry her.

> JAKE
> I believe you should.

70 EXT. DUGOUT – DAY

As Jake and Jack Bull return to the dugout with firewood in their arms, George Clyde awaits them.

71 INT. DUGOUT – DAY

Jake speaks to George Clyde as Jack Bull disposes of the wood.

> JAKE
> Snow's melted. Maybe we should go out on a scout of some sort.

> GEORGE CLYDE
> You are a depository of bad ideas. It could snap cold again at any time.

JAKE

You're staying hot enough at Juanita Willard's.

GEORGE CLYDE

What's that supposed to mean?
(*smiles*)
Aw, don't you worry about me. I'll be ready to ride when the time comes.

72 EXT. DUGOUT – DAY

JACK BULL

Sue Lee will be by this evening.

JAKE

Good. It's been near a week since I've seen her.

JACK BULL

Yes. All this warmth has the Federals out for jaunts. That has kept her home.

JAKE

It won't be long before we join them – out there.

JACK BULL

No it won't. That is why I want to ask something of you and Holt.

JAKE

Name it.

JACK BULL

Well, there, future best man, I would ask you to give us some privacy.

JAKE

Oh you would, would you?

JACK BULL

It's not much to ask.

JAKE

And what are Holt and me to do?

JACK BULL

Anything you'd like. Fling walnuts at squirrels, play
mumblety-peg.

JAKE

I reckon we can come up with a better use of our time than
that, eh, Holt?

HOLT

It is possible.

73 EXT. WOODS – DAY

*Sue Lee walks through the woods. She pauses, listening for something,
but then moves on.*

74 EXT. DUGOUT – DAY

Sue Lee walks up.

SUE LEE

Howdy.

They all greet her.

(*to Holt and Jake*)

I brung you two something.
            (*she pulls something from under her cloak*)
Try this bread, boys.

JAKE

Why thank you. Did you make it?

SUE LEE

No, no. Mrs Evans' sister lives in town. She is a Federal but a
sister still. She gave us two loaves.

JAKE

That is kind of her. Thank her for us, won't you?

She laughs.

SUE LEE

I don't suppose I'll tell her where it went. That might not do.

Jack Bull stands by the dugout door, impatient.

JAKE

Hmm. This good weather has me and Holt wanting to go off
and fling walnuts at mumblety-peg players, or something
along those lines.

JACK BULL

Right. Now have fun.

Sue Lee goes down into the dugout.

(*whispering, holding up a finger*)
Jake. One hour. One hour.

Jake nods to him.

75 EXT. WOODS – DAY

The late-afternoon sun is setting.

*The sack of letters lies in front of Jake's feet. Jake fans out a few letters
in his hand, as if holding a hand of cards. Holt, sitting before him, picks
one.*

JAKE

This thing is addressed to Miss Ruth Ann Jones and it's from
Miss Patricia Foote. 'Dearest Ruth Ann, I trust this letter will
reach you before winter. Here, it is always a sort of winter, as
folks are so cold now. The rebels are out of the city as far as
armies go but there are Copperheads around performing
misdeeds. So much cruelty goes on. Gratiot Prison is full of
rebels and they are left to waste away so pitifully. They are
traitors but also human. If you looked in on them you would
not believe that they were, for they so resemble scarecrows
now. Father believes the war will go on and on, but is ever
more committed to the struggle. He manages to send ever
greater numbers of slaves up north, to freedom and away
from the grasping hands of their masters, who even in the
midst of all attempt to lay claim to them. The Confederates
claim that we strike at their liberty and rights – but what kind
of liberty is it that takes away the liberty of others? The war
will end only when . . . only . . .'

66

Jake's voice trails off at the end. He doesn't look at Holt.

An awkward silence.

> JAKE

You think it's been an hour?

> HOLT

No, the hour ain't gone yet.

Holt takes the loaf of bread and rips it in two, buttering a piece first for Jake and offering it to him.

Jake takes it.

Roedel, do you know my name?

> JAKE

It is Holt.

> HOLT

No, my whole name. My whole name is Daniel Holt, because Daniel is the name my mama gave to me. Daniel, like the lion's den man. Do you know his story?

> JAKE

Of course I do.

> HOLT

That man stood in a lion's den, and he was never ate. But how he come to get out of that den – I never could fix my mind on it.

Holt lets the meaning of this sink in on Jake.

> JAKE
> (*pause*)

Is it an hour now?

> HOLT

Nigh on to it.

At that moment, they hear shots ring out.

> JAKE

The Evanses' place.

Got to be.

They scramble down the slope. The letters remain in a pile on the ground.

76 EXT. DUGOUT – DAY

They come running to the dugout. Jake throws open the plank door and jumps in, warning away Holt from entering.

77 INT. DUGOUT – DAY

Jake discovers Jack Bull quickly dressing and Sue Lee pulling down her skirts – he turns away red-faced, grabbing his and Holt's weapons.

JAKE
Gunshots at the Evanses' place.

JACK BULL
I heard them.

SUE LEE
Oh, Jake.

JAKE
Sue Lee, you stay here. There's going to be a fight.

78 EXT. DUGOUT – DUSK

The boys ride down to the house.

79 EXT. EVANSES' HOUSE – EVENING

They slowly and carefully draw in, hearing shouts and wailing, and catching the light of the burning house.

Mr Evans's body lies in the yard, his wife and daughter crying over him.

MRS EVANS
(*seeing them*)
Oh boys! They killed him, they killed him.

JACK BULL

How many were there?

MRS EVANS

He's dead! He's dead! What will I do?

Jake hears a rider approaching. It's George Clyde, breathless.

GEORGE CLYDE

I heard the fracas all the way from the Willards'. I thought
you boys might be in a spot.

JACK BULL
(*shouting*)

How many?

MRS EVANS

Oh! Oh! A dozen or less.

JAKE

Well, shit, let's get them.

And on down the road they gallop.

80 EXT. ROAD NEAR EVANSES' FARM – DUSK

They ride, almost exuberant. The outlines of the trees blur past them.

81 EXT. ROAD NEAR EVANSES' FARM – NIGHT

Jake trades a glance with Jack Bull as they ride side-by-side. Jack Bull nods and spurs his horse on even faster.

They ride ever faster – right into an ambush.

Flashes of fire break out from behind the hedges on all sides. A group of riders – the infamous 'Red Legs' – rides in to fight at close quarters.

RED LEGS
Traitors! Kill the vermin!

The horses rear and scream. It's pandemonium.

The militia man has Holt in his sights – this time it's Jake's turn to save his comrade. Jake rides in front of him and pegs him at close range. The man falls from his horse and Jake fires again.

DYING MAN
Aw, hell!

Another rider smashes a rifle into Jake's knee.

Jake turns and fires at him.

George Clyde, Holt and Jack Bull all fire away. The militia begins a disorderly retreat, still firing back.

Jake rides up next to Jack Bull, who at that moment lets out a cry – his right arm sprays blood and flaps at his side. He shouts out in pain.

As the Federals retreat, George Clyde dismounts and shoots two of the Red Legs who have fallen, wounded, on the road.

JAKE
Jack Bull is hurt, I've got to get him home.

Jake takes the reins of Jack Bull's horse and leads him back.

82 INT. DUGOUT – NIGHT

Sue Lee sees the injured Jack Bull being brought in. She brings her hand to her mouth to stifle her scream, then gathers her strength and helps Jake lay him down.

JAKE

He'll make it. He'll make it.

The arm is shot to pieces, with cracked bone and tendons trailing out the torn elbow. Jack Bull's eyes have rolled up, leaving only the fluttering whites still visible.

Sue Lee pours water from a jug into a pan, as Jake sets more wood into the fireplace and puts a bowie knife on to the coals.

Sue Lee then goes to Jack Bull and ties his upper arm to stop the flow of blood.

Clyde and Holt enter. Holt takes a look at the arm.

CLYDE

That fire has got to go out.

JAKE

I'm heating water.

GEORGE CLYDE

Heat it quick. They'll come back with more men if they got 'em. We can't have 'em smellin' that fire.

Clyde looks at Jack Bull.

That arm's gonna have to come off.

JAKE

No! We can heal it. He'll need it.

CLYDE

Dutchy, we got no medicine or doctor sense amongst the whole group of us. And I can't go shanghai a sawbones, neither. Federals are likely to be on us by sun-up.

SUE LEE

We'll care for him. I can nurse him with Jake.

GEORGE CLYDE

As you say. But you watch out green rot don't get started on him. Once it does it's over.

72

Holt sits near Jack Bull and watches him closely.

> HOLT
>
> It looks not too good, Jake.

> JAKE
>
> God damn it! Don't nobody say that again!

Jake wraps his hand in a cloth and takes the hot knife in his hands, as Sue Lee washes down Jack Bull's arm.

> Let's see if we can burn the wound closed. Holt.

Holt silently holds down Jack Bull's shoulders.

Jake applies the flat surface of the red-hot knife to Jack Bull's wound and burns it closed. Jack Bull screams, then passes out.

Holt rises.

> HOLT
>
> I'll keep watch.

He walks out of the dugout and pulls the plank closed behind him. George Clyde lies in the corner. Sue Lee and Jake sit on either side of Jack Bull.

---

83 INT. DUGOUT – DAY

Morning light seeps into the dugout.

The raspy breathing of Jack Bull echoes within. Jake sits awake, watching Sue Lee sleep, her head cradled as she holds Jack Bull's good hand, which she has pressed to her lips.

Holt enters, awakening George Clyde and Sue Lee.

> HOLT
>
> They is men on the road.

> GEORGE CLYDE
>
> How many?

> HOLT
>
> More than a few. But they ain't comin' into the woods.

GEORGE CLYDE

Keep the watch. I want to fight away from here if we got to fight.

JAKE

What came of Mrs Evans and Mary?

HOLT

The Willards took them up. They all headed out of here.

GEORGE CLYDE

The Willards too?

HOLT

Said they was goin' south, clear roads or no.

Holt trades a glance with George Clyde, then goes back outside.

Jake sits up, his leg stiff and swollen.

Sue Lee goes and sits next to him.

SUE LEE

He is bad, but how are you feeling?
                    (*beat*)
Your leg, it must hurt.

JAKE

Oh, I been there before.

SUE LEE

Can I help it?

JAKE

Naw. Try to rest yourself.

SUE LEE

I doubt that.

84 EXT. DUGOUT – DAY

Silence. We can barely make out Holt, sitting, watching, in the brush. A light snow falls.

85 EXT. DUGOUT — DUSK

Establishing shot.

86 INT. DUGOUT - DAY

George Clyde sits, alert. Sue Lee and Jake doze.

Jack Bull, delirious, lets out an unintelligible sentence, awakening them.

Sue Lee strokes his forehead, and washes it with a damp cloth.

> GEORGE CLYDE
> Maybe tonight I should try to get us a doctor.

> JAKE
> Where from?

> GEORGE CLYDE
> There is one in Kingsville.

> JAKE
> You can't make it there and back in one night.

> GEORGE CLYDE
> I know that, Dutchy. But I could lay up near there, then try to
> drag him back the next night.

> JAKE
> He may not want to come.

> GEORGE CLYDE
> Oh, I'll reckon he'll come.
> *(gathering his things)*
> If I can't get the doc, I'll head on to Captain Perdee's. Holt'll
> help you and the widow.

> JAKE
> I wish you luck.

George Clyde nods as he heads out.

87 INT. DUGOUT — NIGHT

Holt enters. Jake tosses him a cold potato.

75

JAKE

Dinner.

They all bite into the near-frozen potatoes.

Jake goes over to Jack Bull, who lies, still semi-conscious, on a blanket on the ground.

He takes a bite of his potato, chews it, then spits it out into his palm.

Sue Lee and Holt go to Jack Bull and raise his head, as Jake takes his palm to his friend's mouth and forces the spittle into it.

Jack Bull gags but eventually swallows, and the process is repeated.

They let Jack Bull's head down again.

HOLT
(*softly, to Jake*)
Jake, that arm's done for.

JAKE
Oh, I know it. I hoped it wouldn't be.

HOLT
It is done for.

JAKE
Maybe George will bring the doctor. He may see something we don't.

HOLT
Naw. I reckon he'll see what we see.

JAKE
Not now. We'll give George a chance first.

HOLT
The longer you wait, the harder it gets on the man.

JAKE
Oh hellfire, will you just shut up on that? Holt, just give me peace for a while.

Jack Bull's voice, clear but soft, interrupts them.

JACK BULL

Jake. Jake.

Jake turns to him, then goes to his side.

JAKE

Jack Bull.

JACK BULL

Jake, you look sad.

JAKE

We're takin' care of you. You'll be mended, we're fixin' it.

JACK BULL

Don't lie, Jake. Don't lie. I can see my own arm.

JAKE

George Clyde has gone for a doctor.

JACK BULL
(*nodding*)

I always knew we would be killed. One or both of us. Do you recall the pies on Mother's sill?

JAKE

Of course. Those were good eatin' times.

JACK BULL

That they were.
(*beat*)
I always thought it would be you, Jake. You dying. I was certain I would have to bury you.

JAKE

I wish you were.

JACK BULL

Hah. Me too.

He laughs with a raspy breath. Jake smiles, too, as Jack Bull places his good hand on his knee.

JAKE

You ain't dead, Jack Bull.

77

Sue Lee comes in and goes to them.

JACK BULL

Sue Lee.

SUE LEE

I'm right here.

JACK BULL

Good. That's good.

He closes his eyes and drifts off again. Jake leaves them and joins Holt.

HOLT

Them veins is blackenin', all the way to the armpit. We got to do it now.

SUE LEE
(*grabbing Jake's arm*)

Can you do it?

Jake stands, then walks outside.

88 EXT. DUGOUT – NIGHT

Jake drops to his knees on the frozen ground, retching.

HOLT
(*from behind him*)

Don't think about it, Roedel. Just do it. Just you do it or else I will.

JAKE

Oh no you won't. His family raised me. I reckon it'll be me who saws his rotten arm off.

He walks past Holt back into the dugout.

89 INT. DUGOUT – NIGHT

Jake lashes a rope around the top of Jack Bull's arm and readies the knife.

Holt stands by.

JAKE

If he screams too loud we may all die. Put a stick in his
mouth. Don't let him scream too loud.

He puts it in.

Sue Lee, sit on his chest and keep his jaws clamped on that
stick. Holt, you shove him down wherever he starts to flop.

Jake runs his fingers across Jack Bull's cheek.

*He then steadies himself and starts to saw. The body jerks violently. We
hear Jack Bull's stifled cries as the sawing continues.*

90 EXT. DUGOUT – NIGHT

We hear Jack Bull's muffled cries.

91 EXT. DUGOUT – NIGHT (LATER)

Quiet.

92 INT. DUGOUT – NIGHT

*Holt and Sue Lee stand, exhausted, against a wall, as Jake finishes
digging a shallow grave.*

*He rolls Jack Bull's body into the pit and stands over it, then starts to
push the dirt over him.*

SUE LEE

Wait, Jake. I want to see him.

She goes to the body, leans over it, and kisses the blue lips.

Jake, tentatively, does the same.

*He stands back again, looking down a final time at his dead friend, and
cries.*

Still crying, he finishes burying the body, then tosses down the shovel.

HOLT

We should be gettin' to Captain Perdee's.

JAKE

We got to head south first.
                    (*gesturing to Sue Lee*)
Sue Lee, you'll need a place.
                    (*to Holt*)
We'll go to Browns' farm. Those are Cave Wyatt's people.
They're far away from all this.

Holt nods.

93 EXT. LANDSCAPE – DAY

Holt, Sue Lee and Jake ride off into the snowy night.

94 EXT. WOODED LANE – NIGHT

The snow has picked up. Sue Lee, exhausted, is tied to her horse by Holt and Jake. They keep on.

95 INT. BURNED OUT HOUSE – NIGHT

The three sleep in a corner of the dilapidated and burned structure, the horses tethered nearby.

Jake wraps a blanket around Sue Lee, who sleeps. In her sleep, she curls up to him. He closes his eyes.

96 EXT. BROWN FARM – DAY

Rain falls on a neat, well-tended farmstead.

97 INT. BROWN HOUSE. SITTING ROOM – DAY

It continues to rain. Mrs Brown tends to a feverish Sue Lee, who lies on a couch in the parlor.

Orton Brown sits with Jake and Holt at the adjacent dining-room table, drinking coffee.

Jake, distracted, gets up and walks over to Mrs Brown. He stands awkwardly, watching her minister to Sue Lee.

MRS BROWN

You're not to worry, young man. She'll be just fine. Just give us time.

98 INT. BROWNS' PARLOR – DAY

Jake stands at a window, watching the rain. Sue Lee comes up behind him, looking pale and tired. Jake continues to look at the rain, not noticing her presence. Suddenly, he jumps, and whirls on her.

SUE LEE

Jake. The war hasn't come down here yet.

JAKE

I'm sorry.

SUE LEE

I'm sorry, too.

JAKE

Holt and me. Well, George Clyde should be missin' us –

SUE LEE

You don't have to go back, Jake. Mr Brown says you boys are more than welcome to stay and work the farm. He could use you.

He doesn't respond.

Sue Lee sits and cries. Jake tentatively sits beside her.

JAKE

You'll do all right here.

She nods, tears in her eyes. He rises.

Holt and me'll come by again, just as soon as we can, and see to it.

99 EXT. WOODS – DAY

Jake and Holt ride.

100 EXT. HOG PATH – DAY

Thick brush. We hear rustling, as it parts to reveal Jake and Holt, dead tired, riding slowly through the brush.

Suddenly, the sound of guns cocking into place. A few carbine barrels point out from the trees.

> VOICE
> Who goes there?

> JAKE
> *(almost beyond caring)*
> Who the hell do you think we are?

> VOICE
> You *smell* like a couple of piles of fine southern shit.

From behind the brush, the voice is revealed to be that of George Clyde. He smiles at the two of them.

> GEORGE CLYDE
> Welcome back to hell, boys.

101 EXT. WOODS – DAY

George Clyde, Holt, Riley, Turner and Jake sit and drink. The horses are barely hid in the shed.

> GEORGE CLYDE
> While you boys were sunning yourselves down at the border things have turned rather interesting here.

> TURNER RAWLS
> *(almost indecipherable drawl, from the hole in his cheek)*
> Federals, evuwewear.

> RILEY CRAWFORD
> Welch and his boys got caught in Pattensberg –

> TURNER RAWLS
> *(gesturing)*
> Heads cut off.

GEORGE CLYDE

Some of us still ride. Anderson, Pitt, Todd –

RILEY CRAWFORD

Scalpin' every nigger they can find –
(*noticing Holt*)
– 'cept, of course, our own.

Jake and Clyde both glance at Holt, who seems not to have heard.

GEORGE CLYDE

But there's still riches to be had, right, boys? We've managed
to pluck some prizes from the jaws of death –

TURNER RAWLS

– from dead Federals, at least.

RILEY
(*a bit guiltily*)

If they was Federals.

GEORGE CLYDE

Logically, boys, the fact that they were killed *makes* them
Federals.

Silence. Jake and Holt ponder.

TURNER RAWLS
(*gesturing hand to mouth, to Jake*)

You bring food?

Jake smiles, shakes his head no.

102 EXT. FARM ROAD OFF BONE HILL – DAY

As the group ride warily along, they hear a squealing sound.

*Suddenly, a single pig tears across the road at lightning speed in front of
them and speeds into the woods.*

RILEY CRAWFORD

You see what I see?

He kicks his horse and gives chase to the pig.

GEORGE CLYDE
(*calling after him*)

Riley, hold – aw, hell.

The rest of the men follow.

103 EXT. BONE HILL WOODS – DAY

Riley leads the chase. He comes to a clearing, pulls a pistol, and is about to shoot at the pig, when suddenly a wave of gunfire breaks out from the treeline across the clearing.

Riley turns and heads back into the woods. As he gets to the others a few yards in, he's shot through the gut.

We hear the Federal militia rushing the woods.

RILEY

Aw!

JAYHAWKERS
(*ad lib*)

Kill the secesh!

A good part of Riley's stomach hangs over his belt.

RILEY

I can't ride. Put me down, please. Please put me down.

Jake steps down and pulls the boy off his horse, propping him up against a tree.

Leave me my guns. Don't take 'em. I'll hold 'em.

Turner mouths something indeciperable.

HOLT

Jake!

JAKE
(*cocking a pistol and leaving it*)

You got to fire at them, Riley. Bring them down on you.

RILEY

I will, Jake. I will.

(*crying*)

I was a good boy, wasn't I?

> JAKE
> (*remounting*)
> As good as they come, Riley.

Jake remounts. Turner, Holt, George Clyde and Jake ride back toward the road.

The voices of the Jayhawkers can be heard echoing from everywhere.

> JAYHAWKERS
> (*ad lib*)
> Fan out! Over there!

Then they hear shots, and spur their horses.

> JAKE
> That was Riley! C'mon – follow this gully.

The boys ride off.

Fade to black.

104 INT. FARMHOUSE – NIGHT

The last embers of a fire burn low in the fireplace. The wind rustles a curtain through a broken window. We see the back of the head of a man sitting, quite still, before the fire.

Suddenly, the door bursts open – Jake and Holt push in, guns drawn.

Silence.

They pause, taking the measure of the room, and slowly put their guns back into their belts.

> JAKE
> That the guy we was supposed to shoot?

On the man in the chair, blood-soaked, his neck shot through.

> HOLT
> (*kicking at the fire*)
> Somebody must of got him recent. I'll check back for grub.

He goes to the rear of the house.

Jake idly paces the room, which is in a ghost-like shambles – dusty, overturned furniture. He stumbles on a small drum as he walks over to a writing desk, at which he sits. There's a half-spilled bottle of ink.

JAKE

Holt – we ever been in this house before?

HOLT
(*at the doorway, chewing*)
We been everywhere before. Salt bacon.

JAKE

Hmm.

Jake lays out a sheet of paper, dips the pen, and is about to write something, when he pauses.

JAKE

You know, we were here. With Jack Bull. Man danced a jig right there.

HOLT

You going to write a letter?

JAKE

I was thinkin' of it. But who I got to write to anyhow?

Holt thinks about it.

HOLT

What about that Sue Lee woman? Ain't heard of her since we rode from that farm. You should give her some news. What we been doin'.

JAKE

And what have we done, Holt?
(*pause*)

HOLT

We been stayin' a good step ahead of them Federals, and we ain't been shot down like many –

JAKE
(*throws down the pen*)
Yep. That's what we done. Hell, it ain't worth writing about,
is it?

(*gets up*)

105 EXT. PERDEE ENCAMPMENT – NIGHT

*The flames of a large campfire silhouette the garish figures of drunken
men. Some dance a jig, others stumble, barely able to walk.*

Jake, lying on his bed-clothes, looks on, dejected. Holt lies asleep nearby.

106 EXT. PERDEE ENCAMPMENT – NIGHT

*A card game in progress. In the background, we see Black John sitting,
staring menacingly into space. Cave talks casually to Jake as they play.*

CAVE WYATT
Best to stay clear of Black John right now. You know when
that women's jail collapsed in Kansas City, his womenfolk
were in it – three of them, done in by the Federals. He's actin'
kinda itchy, if you know what I mean –

PITT MACKESON
I'll see you and raise you.

ANDERSON
I am short of cash – will these do?

He tosses two scalps into the pot.

TODD
That's two nigger scalps – I'll see you with one Dutch scalp.

Cave Wyatt looks uncomfortable.

CAVE WYATT
I'm out of this one.

He folds his cards, as does Jake. They trade glances.

TURNER RAWLS
I just got money.

87

PITT MACKESON
Don't worry, Turner, we'll take your money.

Todd and Anderson laugh.

107 EXT. PERDEE ENCAMPMENT – DAY

Bushwhackers stream into the camp, joining nearly a hundred men, Jake included, who are already there. They follow as a tall, handsome man – the famous rebel guerrilla Quantrill – strides across the camp.

MEN
(*ad lib*)
What's he got on his mind? Quantrill – I knew he'd be back!

108 EXT. PERDEE CAMP – NIGHT

Jake sees Quantrill huddling with his lieutenants.

109 EXT. PERDEE ENCAMPMENT – DAY

As we move through the crowd, we hear cheers, and the sounds of speechifying.

At the head of the group, Quantrill stands on a wagon bed and addresses the men.

QUANTRILL
Men of the South! Our enemies are sleeping. Just as our sisters slept in that Kansas City jail until the walls fell down and crushed the breath right out of them. Good women whose lives were cut short by Yankee treachery. But now our Southern sisters' souls fly forth to transmogrify into the fire and steel that will destroy our enemies! Yes, my boys, the abolitionists of Lawrence sleep under the heavy blanket of guilt that covers their shame. The black Republicans of Lawrence, Kansas, sleep heavily under the gathering clouds of our vengeance. But we shall awaken them one last time, and we shall fill their eyes with terror, and send them to eternal slumber! To Lawrence, boys. Over the border!

The mingling bands of guerrillas, desperadoes and Bushwhackers raise a hurrah. Quantrill continues.

110 EXT. PERDEE ENCAMPMENT – NIGHT

The camp is being broken down as the men pack up.

Jake looks nervous. He walks over to George Clyde.

> JAKE
>
> George, Lawrence is some fifty miles into Kansas. There are whole armies out there and no friends at all.

> GEORGE CLYDE
> (*jovial*)
>
> You got it, Dutchy. You know as well as I do that we'll never make it to Lawrence. But we'll sure as hell go down fighting on those prairies.

> CAVE WYATT
>
> Maybe a couple of us will bust through all the way to Lawrence, George – what do you say? I sure hope I make it, 'cause I plan on givin' that town some memories before they kill me.

Around them, the whiskey is flowing – bands of already drunk and dangerous-looking men are whooping it up, singing, gambling, wrestling.

Jake walks through the almost surreal scene as more men arrive in the camp.

He comes upon Holt, working the camp kitchen with two other black men, Nolan and Wilson. They seem cowed and anxious.

Jake calls to him.

> JAKE
> Holt – come on over and share some busthead.

Holt trades glances with his black companions.

> HOLT
> I got work back here to finish.

Jake realizes Holt's predicament.

> JAKE
> Well, when you're finished up then.

As Jake turns, he unexpectedly bumps into George Clyde and Pitt Mackeson.

> PITT MACKESON
> You two sure got to be pals, didn't you? Ever since you came back you two boys have been clapping your gums together regular as crones.

Jake just pushes by Pitt. George Clyde gives Holt an ambivalent look, as Holt goes back about his business.

III EXT. PERDEE ENCAMPMENT – DAY

The drunk and hung-over fighters – now 300 strong – leave the encampment and head for Kansas.

Some of the loudest drunks congregate to the rear of the line, singing.

Holt rides up and silently joins Jake.

112 EXT. DESERTED LANDSCAPE – DAY

A hot dusty day – the riders move through the devastated landscape of Western Missouri. They pass whiskey bottles around.

Cave Wyatt, Turner Rawls, George Clyde, Jake and Holt share a bottle as they ride.

113 EXT. ROAD – DAY

The riders move on.

114 EXT. KANSAS ROAD – DAY

The column travels on.

115 EXT. KANSAS CREEKSIDE – DUSK

Some of the horses are being watered. Quantrill and his lieutenants enforce silence among the men.

> LIEUTENANT
> Hush up, boys. There's a Federal post just over the ridge.

116 EXT. KANSAS WOODS – DUSK

The men sit on horseback, whispering, waiting for a signal to continue moving.

A guerrilla ahead raises his arm and signals the men forward.

117 EXT. KANSAS/MISSOURI BORDER – DAY

A Bushwacker Scout halts before an encampment of fresh Confederate recruits. Their Captain addresses the Scout.

> CAPTAIN
> These boys ain't seen much in the way of fightin' yet, but we heard you were headin' over to Kansas. We are willing to meet the enemy as part of Colonel Quantrill's ranks.

The Scout looks unimpressed.

> SCOUT
> Well, wake these children up. I suppose we can use them as cannon fodder.

118 EXT. KANSAS/MISSOURI BORDER – DAY

As the combined troop travels on, they pass a group of farmers who watch them go by, then join them at the rear of the column, hurrahing 'Lawrence!'

Jake turns and watches as they join.

> JAKE
> Fools. Those farmers wouldn't be able to fight a herd of cattle, let alone the Kansas Fifth.

> HOLT
> No more fools than you and me, Jake.

119 EXT. KANSAS FARMLAND – NIGHT

As the tired column moves slowly and silently forward – Bushwackers first, then Confederate recruits, then farmers – Holt stands, tying the drowsy Jake to his horse. He then gets on his horse and pulls Jake along.

120 EXT. KANSAS FARMLAND – NIGHT

Quantrill and Black John ride up and down the line urging everyone to pick up speed.

> QUANTRILL
> Ride on, men! We can make it there before sun-up!

Jakes's eyes flutter closed. Cave shoves him on the back.

> CAVE WYATT
> Sweet dreams, Dutchy? Ah, go back to sleep – you just may wake up in Lawrence tomorrow.

121 EXT. THE ROAD TO LAWRENCE – DAY

The sun rises behind the bleary-eyed riders.

Lawrence, with Mount Oread towering behind it, stretches before them – tidy grids of streets, treeless, glinting in the sun.

> JAKE
> We made it. We made it. There she is.

Quantrill has gathered his lieutenants around him and is calmly giving orders.

> QUANTRILL
> We'll form into fours. Your boys should set up a post on
> Mount Oread. Watch the road from Fort Leavenworth.
> *(handing out lists to different men)*
> Here's the death list – we will cross off every name. That's
> Berkeley Street there – first to Jim Lane's house! I'm taking
> Scott, you, the rest to the Eldridge House. Let's move.

The men slowly advance, silent.

122 EXT. ELMORE HOUSE – DAY

A middle-aged man, still in his night shirt, walks out of his house. He yawns, and squints at the eastern sun in his eyes, stopping dead in his tracks. Before him – Quantrill and his 300 raiders.

The horsemen and the man stand motionless and silent before each other, for what seems like an eternity. No one appears to know what to do.

From among the ranks, Pitt Mackeson slides off his horse. He walks deliberately up to the man, lifts his pistol, and shoots the man in the face.

123 EXT. ELMORE HOUSE – DAY

The raiders let up a cry, spurring their horses.

124 EXT. LAWRENCE OUTSKIRTS – DAY

The raiders begin to ride in to town, first slowly, and then at a gallop.

125 EXT. RECRUITMENT CAMP – DAY

The Captain and a couple of recruits emerge groggily from their tents, unsure of the meaning of the distant noises they hear.

126 EXT. LAWRENCE OUTSKIRTS – DAY

CLOSE ON *first Jake, then Holt, then Black John, riding furiously amid the raiders.*

127 EXT. ROAD BEFORE RECRUITMENT CAMP – DAY

We track with the raiders entering town, ending at the encampment with Quantrill in the foreground.

> QUANTRILL
> Kill, boys, kill! Make no mistake!

Black John fires and hits the Captain of the recruits, and the other raiders let loose with a murderous volley as they charge into the white tents of the encampment, which are immediately sprayed red with blood.

128 EXT. MASSACHUSSETTS STREET – DAY

Two hundred raiders charge down Lawrence's main street. We see them from various angles.

As the group rides up, small clusters of men begin to peel off, entering stores and buildings, dragging sleepy men outside and shooting them.

129 EXT. MASSACHUSSETTS AND 8TH STREETS – DAY

Holt, Jake and four other raiders turn off in to a residential area.

130 EXT. MASSACHUSSETTS STREET – DAY

From the boardwalk, we pan to see the tail end of the rush, and see raiders dragging men out of buildings.

131 EXT. BACK OF MASSACHUSSETTS STREET – DAY

We follow Babe Hudspeth riding, as in the background men rush out of buildings.

132 EXT. BACK OF MASSACHUSSETTS STREET – DAY

A woman holds on to the reins of a raider's horse as the raider tries to give chase to her husband.

133 EXT. ELDRIDGE HOUSE – DAY

Quantrill and some men ride up. He shouts up to the upper stories.

QUANTRILL

Eldridge! Surrender now or suffer the consequences.

A white sheet is waved from a window – the raiders let up a shout.

134 EXT. NEWSPAPER OFFICE – DAY

Skaggs, a particularly nasty raider, drags Mr Spear out on to the street, followed by Spear's wife and twelve-year-old son. Skaggs pushes the son to the ground and shoots Spear.

135 EXT. MASSACHUSSETTS STREET/LAND AGENCY OFFICE – DAY

George Clyde rides slowly down the street. In the background men are being chased down. Jogging along beside his horse is a townsman, Dulinski, who addresses him in a Polish accent, although George appears to be paying him no mind.

DULINSKI

When I arrive, who was I not to know this town is full to brim of Northern abolitionaries! I am sickened – yes! But now real southern men is coming, and I say hooray, as I am southern man in heart. Perhaps you join for whiskey – here – I have in office.

He gestures at the land agency office they are just passing.

GEORGE CLYDE

Whiskey?

DULINSKI

Ah yes!

George Clyde stops his horse.

136 EXT. FITCH HOUSE – DAY

As two raiders drag Fitch out of his house, Turner Rawls addresses him.

TURNER RAWLS

Wha is Majo Gubbs?

FITCH

What? What did you say?

TURNER RAWLS

Whar ees Majo Gwubbs?

FITCH

Pardon?

TURNER RAWLS

Aw!

Turner, in frustration, takes out his pistol and empties it into Fitch, then takes out another gun and does the same. Fitch's wife lets out a scream.

137 EXT. RIGGS HOUSE — DAY

Jake and another raider drag Riggs out of his house, as Holt stands beside Mrs Riggs. As the other raider is about to shoot Riggs, his wife pushes his arm and he misfires. Riggs makes a run for it as the raider continues to shoot after him. Riggs falls in the street and the raider raises a shout and mounts his horse.

RAIDER

You boys fire up the house.

138 EXT. STREET IN FRONT OF RIGGS HOUSE — DAY

Mrs Riggs runs down the street, hysterical, and falls on to the prostrate body of her husband.

139 EXT. SCHOOLHOUSE — DAY

Skaggs, drinking from a bottle, wheels and turns on his horse in front of the schoolhouse, which is beginning to burn.

140 EXT. MASSACHUSSETTS STREET — DAY

A stunned man stands, dazed, in the middle of the street, as all around him the murder and mayhem ensues. The beginnings of smoke and fire from one or two buildings can be seen in the background.

Black John rides by and then wheels back around.

BLACK JOHN

Look at you cowards! Where is your army? Who have we to fight? You are cowards all!

The man simply stares, vacant.

141 EXT. FITCH HOUSE – DAY

The house is on fire, as Mrs Fitch runs out holding a framed photograph of her husband. Turner wrests it from her arms and throws it back into the fire.

142 EXT. STREET IN FRONT OF RIGGS HOUSE – DAY

Mrs Riggs is still crying over her husband's body. Suddenly she stops herself, amazed.

> MR RIGGS
> (*whispering*)
> Now, woman, calm yourself. I simply tripped, and can't say as I'm shot anywheres anyhow.

She looks up to see smoke coming out of their house, with Jake and Holt exiting it.

> MRS RIGGS
> Oh God – the house.

She leaps up and runs back to the house, leaving him lying on the ground.

143 EXT. STREET IN FRONT OF RIGGSES' HOUSE – DAY

Riggs looks up after his wife, only to see Turner coming, with Cave following close behind.

He gets up and runs – Turner sees him and gives chase.

144 EXT. RIGGSES' HOUSE – DAY

Mrs Riggs runs from her well with a bucket of water and into her house, as Holt and Jake stand in front of it.

> JAKE
> Shall we stop her?

> HOLT
> We just s'posed to set it. Not my business what she do now.

They walk away.

145 EXT. EIGHTH STREET – DAY

Jake and Holt walk towards the Eldridge Hotel. They witness more fire.

They pass the storehouse where raiders are loading up wagons.

146 INT. FISHER HOUSE. PARLOR – DAY

Riggs bursts into the Fisher parlor, where his sister Mary and an older woman, Aunt Grace, are standing.

> RIGGS
> Sister, you must hide me.

Auntie Grace picks up a straight razor and gestures.

> AUNT GRACE
> Back in here, quick!

They run into another room.

147 INT. FISHER HOUSE. PARLOR — DAY

Moments later.

Turner bursts into the parlor.

> **TURNER**
> Wheh is bastah!

> **MARY FISHER**
> He ran out the back.

Turner pulls his gun.

> **TURNER**
> I go lookin'.

148 INT. FISHER HOUSE. BEDROOM — DAY

The door bursts open as Turner swings into the room, gun drawn.

His POV: Aunt Grace standing next to a rather old woman crouched in a wheelchair, shivering, in a makeshift dress with a bonnet over her head. It's Riggs, his mustache newly-shaved off.

> **TURNER**
> Huh.

> **AUNT GRACE**
> It's just me and Granny Esther.

> **TURNER**
> Oh.

As Turner turns to go; Cave comes up behind him.

> **CAVE**
> Best get these old folks out, as this place is gonna burn.

Cave does a double take on 'Granny Esther's' hairy fingers, but doesn't say anything.

149 INT. LAND AGENCY OFFICE — DAY

As George Clyde looks out the window, he sees Bushwackers shooting objects off the heads of a group of men lined up across the street. He drinks pensively from a glass of whiskey as Dulinski drones on, paying him no heed. Smoke from various fires drifts across the street.

DULINSKI

Sure, that Jim Lane, he steal the slaves. But he just sell them again another day. Me, yes, I always do what I can for the cause, even when it is so hard because of living here in Lawrence. Not too many people like me here in this town, no sir.

150 EXT. NEWSPAPER OFFICE – DAY

Mrs Spear and her son cover the body of Mr Spear with a blanket as Skaggs rides by, an American flag tied to his horse's tail. The boy watches Skaggs.

151 EXT. ELDRIDGE HOTEL – DAY

As Jake and Holt approach, a group of men mill around the hotel. From the third floor, a man is thrown from a window by a pair of raiders. The group below shoots at his body as it flies down to the street.

They step under the awnings and see Quantrill going over a map of the town, handing out quiet commands to a group around him.

152 INT./EXT. GENERAL STORE – DAY

George Clyde enters – Dulinski with him – and addresses one of the scared store clerks.

GEORGE CLYDE

Give me that pipe up there. And some tobacco.

The Clerk fetches it as, all around him, raiders can be seen grabbing items off the shelves.

Skaggs, on horseback in front of store, firing his gun drunkenly in the air, falls off his horse through the window, in a drunken sleep.

George Clyde walks by him on his way out.

DULINSKI

You think he is OK?

RAIDER

He'll sleep it off.

153 EXT. ELDRIDGE HOTEL – DAY

Holt and Jake are joined by a pair of elderly Southern men, farmer volunteers, who look on the scene sadly.

Gunfire and screams can be heard from upstairs.

SOUTHERN GENTLEMAN #1

We had thought this would be a real fight. But it – it's just –

JAKE

– It's just bad-luck citizens, finding out just how bad luck can be.

SOUTHERN GENTLEMAN #2

They ought not to murder the young ones.

JAKE
(half-heartedly)

But pups make hounds.

If it was your pup, you'd feel different, son.

Jake nods. They hear more gunfire, and see two black men being executed across the street.

> JAKE
>
> Holt. Let's get us some eggs.

> HOLT
>
> Yes, Jake. Let's get us all the eggs they got, and some ham, too.

They walk out on to the street, the two old men with them.

154 EXT. ELDRIDGE HOTEL – DAY

As Jake, Holt and the two elderly Southerners walk on to the street, a passing Raider throws Holt up against a wall.

Holt violently pushes him off, but Jake restrains Holt from taking a swing at him.

> JAKE
> (*to the Raider*)
> You fool. This man's with us!

The drunk Raider doesn't seem to understand.

> DRUNK RAIDER
>
> Huh?

> JAKE
>
> It's George Clyde's nigger, you fool.

The Raider stumbles off.

Holt disengages from Jake. The group walks on.

155 EXT. LAWRENCE HOUSE – DAY

Jake and the group stop in front of a small boarding house, and walk up the stairs and enter it.

Inside, they are met by an Elderly Woman wearing an apron, shaking with fear. Crouching in a corner of the dining-room are an old man and a young boy.

                              JAKE
You were makin' breakfast there?

                         ELDERLY WOMAN
Yes.

                              JAKE
What were you makin'?

                         ELDERLY WOMAN
Taters.

                              JAKE
And coffee?

                         ELDERLY WOMAN
Yes.

                              JAKE
Let's have some breakfast.

Jake nonchalantly pulls a chair from the table, pretending not even to notice the old man and boy quaking right next to him.

The others take their seats, as the Elderly Woman begins to serve them.

The sounds of gunfire, screaming and fire can be heard from outside.

The men continue eating in silence.

                             OLD MAN
Mister –

                              JAKE
Shut up. More coffee, if you please, ma'am.

Just then, the front door bursts open and Pitt Mackeson, accompanied by a gang of drunk and bloodthirsty Raiders, runs in.

PITT MACKESON

Jake Roedel! Bring those two outside. I want to show them something.

JAKE

Morning, Pitt. We'll see to them once we've had our vittles.

Pitt takes this in.

PITT MACKESON

Why, you little Dutch son of a bitch. You do what I tell you. Or I'll kill you.

Jake, with a cup of coffee at his lips, swiftly pulls his pistol with his other hand and points it at Pitt's face.

JAKE

And when you figure to do this mean thing to me, Mackeson? Is this very moment convenient for you? It is for me.

A long silence.

Dave, one of Pitt's men, pushes forward.

DAVE

Let's just take 'em out.

One of the old gents, Rufus Stone, stands.

RUFUS STONE

No, that won't work.

The other gent stands too.

PITT MACKESON

Aw, the hell with it. There's plenty other Jayhawkers to kill.

He turns a step, then whirls around, a finger pointing at Jake.

I'll see you back in Missouri, you tiny sack of shit.

JAKE

You know where to find me.

Pitt and his gang leave.

Jake gives off a fake yawn, and sits back down.

RUFUS STONE

That's Pitt Mackeson, ain't it? I hear he'd as soon as kill a man as mash a tick.

JAKE

My, what a scary fellow he is.

Rufus Stone smiles appreciatively.

RUFUS STONE

I like you, son. But that bastard will have your scalp if you ain't careful.

Jake, chewing, looks over at Holt. They know their days, if not hours, are numbered.

The Old Man breaks his silence.

OLD MAN

Thank you mister, thank you – there ain't enough thanks in the world –

JAKE

Aw, you go to hell!

Jake rises, as does Holt.

Thank you, ma'am. Good day.

157 INT./EXT. BOARDING HOUSE – DAY

Through the boarding house window, we see that the guerrillas are starting to head out.

RAIDER #1
(*riding quickly, waving his hat*)
Federal cavalry eight miles off! Pack up, boys!

158 EXT. BOARDING HOUSE – DAY

As Jake and Holt emerge, another post rides by.

RAIDER #2
Move on, men, before the Yankees get here! Move out!

There is smoke everywhere.

159 EXT. STABLES – DAY

Cave Wyatt gets horses.

160 EXT. FITCH HOUSE – DAY

Mrs Fitch watches her house in flames. A raider comes by and takes off her husband's boots.

161 EXT. ELDRIDGE HOTEL – DAY

Jake and Holt walk, through crowds of departing raiders, back across to the hotel, which is up in flames. There are bodies everywhere.

Cave Wyatt rides up behind them with a pair of extra horses.

CAVE WYATT
Fresh horses, boys. You'd best saddle up on these.

He gives them a meaningful look, looks around.

And you'd best ride in the back of the column. They're sayin' words on you.

Jake and Holt trade glances.

> (*quietly*)
> You did right. I did the same, it's just no one knows it on me. Some of the boys have got to talking, and, well, we're thinking of slipping down to Arkansas, to join up with the regulars, get out of this. You want to come?

JAKE

When are you going?

CAVE WYATT

Well, that's not set. We'll leave from camp, maybe tomorrow. If we make it back.

162 EXT. GENERAL STORE – DAY

Jake and Holt pass by Clyde sitting on the stoop in front of the store with Dulinski.

HOLT

George.

Clyde barely acknowledges them, but gets up.

163 EXT. GENERAL STORE – DAY

As George Clyde remounts to leave, Dulinski pipes up.

DULINSKI

So long, raider man! You are Southern heroes, and I, I will always remember Southern friends who have come here today! Good friends, yes. Thank you, good morning!

George, on his horse, pauses, disgusted, and turns back on Dulinski, pulling his gun and shooting him in the chest. He then rides on.

164 EXT. MASSACHUSSETTS STREET – DAY

The raiders, some pulling wagons stuffed with plunder, others on horses weighed down with goods, leave the smoldering and burning town.

165 INT. GENERAL STORE – DAY

Skaggs, asleep and left behind, slowly comes to as he feels someone pulling his revolver from his hand. We see that it is young Spear, who now fumbles with the gun.

> SKAGGS
>
> What the . . . ?

He sees the boy trying to get the gun to work, and raises himself, drawing another pistol from his belt.

Just as he draws, the boy's gun goes off, killing Skaggs.

166 EXT. MASSACHUSSETTS STREET – DAY

Wide shot of the raiders, leaving Lawrence.

167 EXT. ROAD – DAY

The riders are more drunk and tired than ever. Most can barely stay in their saddle. Some ride horses hitched to carts overflowing with plunder. Black John and Quantrill's lieutenants ride along the line, urging them to move on quickly.

168 EXT. TOP OF MASSACHUSSETTS STREET – DAY

Lawrence is now a city only of women – some weeping, others helping the wounded and the grieving. In the background, the town destroyed.

169 EXT. ROAD – DAY

Black John and George Clyde ride along the column towards the back. They halt when they come to Jake.

> BLACK JOHN
> I heard disappointing words on you, Roedel.

> JAKE
> Is that so?

> BLACK JOHN
> Are you a traitor, Roedel?

> JAKE
> You know I ain't.

> BLACK JOHN
> Well, you spared, boy. I told you not to spare.

Just then, two rebel Riders come up from the rear, their horses lathered.

RIDER

Whoa! Federal troops, sir. Closing behind.

Black John gives Jake a final look, and rides off to help organize the line.

George Clyde stays on.

GEORGE CLYDE

I'll do what I can for you.

He rides off.

170 EXT. ROAD – DAY

Quantrill is organizing the men.

QUANTRILL

We'll cut down this way, boys.

171 EXT. ROAD – DAY

The raiders are roadlocked behind a broken wagon. Black John rides up.

BLACK JOHN

No way through here. Let me charge them with my boys.

172 EXT. NARROWING ROAD – DAY

Federal cavalry rides forward, determined and swift, but unaware of what's about to meet them. Ahead of them, a Federal scout comes tearing back.

The Federal column halts.

FEDERAL CAPTAIN

What is it?

At that moment, the chilling sound of hundreds of rebels, trilling, yelling, screaming, emerging from the woods on foot – everywhere.

Oh hell! By company, into line, boys!

The Federals line up and commence firing.

A few of the rebels fall, but the charge continues.

173 EXT. MEADOW – DAY

We see the rebels, some with rifles, most with pistols, moving forward. They pause to form a line, and fire.

Jake, Cave Wyatt, Babe Hudspeth and Holt are among them.

174 EXT. FEDERAL LINE – DAY

The Federals are badly hit.

> FEDERAL CAPTAIN
> Pull back to the tree line! Pull back!

175 EXT. MEADOW – DAY

The rebels give a victorious shout. A second line – some men on horseback, others walking horses – moves up. Cave is walking up a few horses.

Fire again!

There is scattered shooting.

Jake and Holt take aim and fire repeatedly.

They hear gunfire from behind them and spin around.

It's Pitt Mackeson and two of his men.

As they turn to face them, we hear a huge wave of shouting from the Federal line – the Yankees have regrouped and are charging!

They've regrouped! Here they come!

A sea of bullets flies into the rebel line.

Behind Jake we can see the outlines of the Federal troops taking formation.

Bullets are flying everywhere. Horses are scattering.

Holt takes aim at Pitt, but is struck by a bullet that passes through his side. He yells and staggers, falling to his knees.

George Clyde rides over to him and gets off his horse. As he braces himself to lift Holt, he takes a bullet straight through the neck, collapsing into Holt's arms. Holt stares into his eyes as the light goes out of them, chaos all around.

Jake gets a shot off, then turns to see Holt fall to the ground with George Clyde, and is hit himself in the leg by a shot from Pitt Mackeson.

As Pitt disappears behind a rush of men and smoke, Jake limps after him, screaming insanely.

JAKE
Where are you, Pitt? I'll kill you! I'm gonna kill you, Pitt! I'm gonna kill you!

In the chaos, Cave Wyatt comes up on horseback.

He disengages Holt, still madly clinging to George Clyde, and gets him up on a horse.

Another man rides over to Jake and helps him up also.

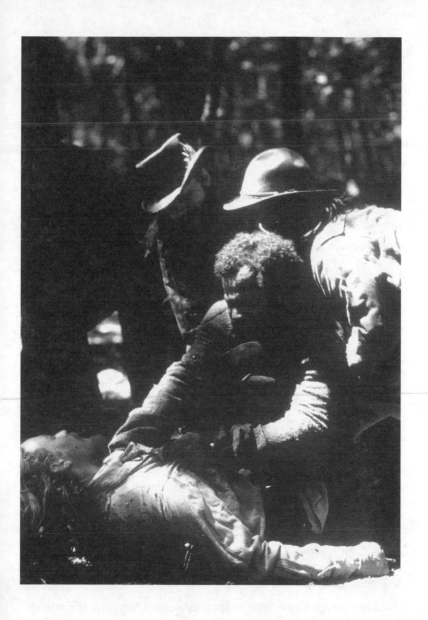

CAVE WYATT
C'mon!

JAKE
No – lemme kill him! Lemme kill him!

Cave, holding the reins to Holt's horse, rides off with Jake through the mêlée, as Jake still screams madly after Pitt.

176 EXT. ROAD – NIGHT

Jake, Holt and Cave Wyatt ride along.

Jake's pant leg is bright red and moist.

Holt is in pain with each horse-step, but holds it in.

Jake looks over to Holt, who averts his gaze.

177 EXT. RIVER BANK – DAY

Holt stands beside his horse, weak from loss of blood, staring into the water.

In the background, Cave helps lift Jake up on to his horse, having finished a makeshift bandage on his leg. Jake rides cautiously up to Holt.

Holt turns to Jake. We see that he has been crying.

JAKE
We'll make for the Brown farm.
(*nodding to Holt's bloody side*)
Can you make it?

Holt doesn't respond.

You're gonna make it. OK?

He reins his horse and pulls away.

178 EXT. BROWNS' FARM – DAY

The men ride up. Cave helps Jake off his horse. Orton and Wilma Brown come to the front door.

Jake sits with difficulty down on to a bench. Holt is eased down next to him by Cave Wyatt.

ORTON

Welcome back, son.

JAKE

I appreciate this of you.

ORTON

I don't think you know just how much you *do* appreciate it.

Jake and Holt don't quite catch his drift.

We'll set you boys up in the parlor here.

CAVE WYATT

Much obliged, Ort. I'll just be stayin' the night.

They leave Jake and Holt for a bit. As Wilma works in the kitchen, she gives the boys an occasional odd glance. Cave and Orton can be seen whispering in the kitchen.

Jake and Holt just sit in silence.

Sue Lee enters the house. She is radiant, and not at all flustered to see Jake again.

SUE LEE
(*to Jake*)

Are you hurt again?

JAKE

Well, yes. But I didn't do it to myself, you know. Me and Holt, we been shot.

SUE LEE

Well, you should have expected it.

JAKE

I hear you saying it.

Just then, a cry can be heard from the kitchen.

Jake and Holt sit up as though they've heard a ghost.

115

The cry is repeated, preternatural, insistent.

Sue Lee matter-of-factly marches into the kitchen, and reappears a moment later, holding a baby in her arms. Wilma, Orton and Cave crowd around the door behind her, watching the dumbstruck Jake and Holt.

SUE LEE

Well, what do you think of her? Her name is Grace – Grace Shelley Chiles, as far as I'm concerned.

Jake and Holt look up at the baby in wonder, tears in their eyes. They nod, not knowing really what to do.

HOLT

Okay.

JAKE

Looks all right to me.

Jake and Holt look at each other, nod again.

Sue Lee puts the baby on the floor.

SUE LEE

Let me take a look at your bad spot, Jake. I want to make sure it's clean.

JAKE

Oh, it's clean enough.

SUE LEE

No, Jake. Clean enough ain't good enough. You should know that. And you too, Holt, let me take a look.

Jake, embarrassed, lets her tend to his leg, as the baby crawls back to Wilma.

180 EXT. BROWNS' HOUSE – MORNING

Cave's horse, saddled, paws the ground.

181 INT. BROWNS' HOUSE. PARLOR – DAY

Jake and Holt stand awkwardly, as Cave rises to depart.

JAKE

Thank you, Cave.

CAVE

Maybe when you're fixed up you come down and join the
regulars with me.

JAKE

Maybe that.

Cave pauses at the door.

CAVE

Ort tells me that when you brung that girl here she was
already pregnant. You better marry her, boy. It ain't right not
to.

JAKE

Me? No, not me. I don't got to marry nobody.

CAVE

Is that right? You're that kind of man, Dutchy?

JAKE

I will take care of her, Cave. It'll be took care of somehow.
When it can be.

CAVE

That's all I ask. Everybody likes her real good, you know. Ort
and Wilma, they already think of her as something of a
daughter.

JAKE

That's good to hear.

182 INT. BROWNS' HOUSE. PARLOR – NIGHT

Holt and Jake are bedded down. Holt tosses, obviously annoying Jake.

JAKE

Well?

HOLT

Could be you ought to.

JAKE

Ought to what?

HOLT

I've thunk it from several sides, and could be she'd make you a fine wife.

JAKE

But there is one 'lil thing we ain't mentioning here. It might just be she don't *want* to marry me. That is, even if I *did* want to marry her.

183 EXT. BROWNS' HOUSE. PORCH – DAY

Jake and Holt sit and watch the others go about their tasks.

JAKE

How's your rib?

HOLT

None too good. How's your leg?

JAKE

Same.

HOLT

Hmm.

Sue Lee comes and sits next to Jake.

SUE LEE

I have a thing or two to say to you, Jake.

JAKE

Well, speak up.

HOLT

I think I want a walk.

He gets up slowly and goes back into the house.

SUE LEE

Jake, what's this trash I hear about you being my fiancée?

JAKE

Oh, so you've heard that. Well, it was sprung on me by Cave.

See, they all seem to think you was carrying my kid because I, well, after Jack Bull, I brought you here.

SUE LEE

Ah.

(*beat*)

Do you figure I ought to be married?

JAKE

Yes, if you want to keep fingers from waggin' in your face.

SUE LEE

Oh, that doesn't bother me.

JAKE

Well, it's also another thing, Sue Lee. They got a name for kids without daddies, you know. It's not a good one.

SUE LEE

I know that. So, do *you* want to marry me?

JAKE

Naw. Not too bad.

SUE LEE

(*beat*)

Good. That's good news. 'Cause I wouldn't marry you for a wagonload of gold.

JAKE

I bet you wouldn't.

SUE LEE

I wouldn't marry you even if you weren't a runty Dutchman with a nubbin for a finger.

JAKE

Fine! That's damned fine. I wouldn't want a wife who didn't keep her place. Anyhow, it is a proven thing that being your man is just plain bad luck, and I don't need to marry any of that.

A pause.

SUE LEE
(*quietly*)
Well, it's true. I guess it's true.

Another pause.

JAKE
Aw, you're not bad luck. You've just had bad luck, that's all.

She picks up the baby, who's been on the floor.

SUE LEE
I'd need convincing that you mean that. And I'd need convincing that you were right.

She takes the child and goes inside.

184 INT. BROWNS' HOUSE. DINING ROOM – DAY

Holt and Jake are finishing breakfast. Wilma takes Holt's plate.

HOLT
Thank you, ma'am.

WILMA
You're welcome.

She goes into the yard.

Holt rises gingerly.

HOLT
I'll catch some air.

JAKE
Breathe some for me.

Jake slides his way to a warm spot in front of the window.

Sue Lee enters with the baby, putting her down.

SUE LEE
Perhaps you boys can see after this little one while I'm at my chores.

Jewel with director Ang Lee

HOLT
(*smiling, as he leaves*)
Maybe it's best you talk to Jake about that line of work, Miss.

JAKE
Who, me?

SUE LEE
That's right. It's about time you were of some help around here. I'll be back by noontime.

JAKE
Wait –

She's off.

Jake slides over to the baby.

He looks quizzically at her. No response. He makes a small baby face – she erupts, screaming like a banshee.

Ah, hell!

185 EXT. BROWNS' HOUSE – DAY

We hear the sound of the baby screaming.

186 INT. BROWNS' HOUSE – DAY

Jake sits by the window as the baby screams and screams.

> JAKE
>
> Now come on!

He picks her up. The screaming only intensifies.

Holt sits across the room, laughing.

> HOLT
>
> She's louder than a gut-shot Yankee.

He gets up and walks to the door.

> JAKE
>
> Hey, where you going?

Holt just laughs.

187 INT. BROWN HOUSE – DAY

The baby's still screaming. Jake's making carnival faces at here, but to no avail.

He puts her on his knee and jiggles her. Still screaming.

He waves his hand in front of her. No good.

He caresses her cheek. Suddenly, her lips curl around his nubbined pinkie. Silence.

> JAKE
> (smiling)
>
> I knew that nubbin was good for something.

Sue Lee enters.

> Where you been? She's been screaming for an hour.

> SUE LEE
>
> Sweet thing wants some suck, but Momma's been busy.
> Here, I'll feed her.

JAKE

Hell, no, you won't. I've just now got this thing under
control.

SUE LEE

She needs to be suckled, Jake.

JAKE

Ah hell.

*Sue Lee takes the baby and sits in a rocking-chair on the other side of
the parlor, cradling the baby to her chest. Paying Jake no heed, she
unbuttons her blouse, revealing a breast, and puts the baby to it.*

SUE LEE

Here now.

She looks up over at Jake. Jake just sits there, looking.

Then he slides across the floor a bit to get a closer look.

188 INT. BROWNS' PARLOR – NIGHT

*Babe Hudspeth has come for a visit. He drinks coffee with Orton, Jake
and Holt.*

BABE

They're all busted up.

JAKE

Quantrill.

BABE

Headed to Kentucky.

JAKE

Anderson?

BABE

Dead, I've heard tell. Thrailkill, Clement, most of 'em dead.

HOLT

Pitt Mackeson?

BABE

He's got hisself something of a gang. But these days they

spend most of their time robbin' for plunder, and they don't care whether they take it from Southern folks or Federals. Anyone gets in their way –

          (*gesturing over his forehead*)

– off comes their scalp.

Holt and Jake trade glances.

Anyhow, they don't ride much in Jackson or Cass counties no more. Word has it they're headin' south – they'll probably make you a visit.

          (*looking at Jake*)

Word is they're making a plan of it, Jake.

189 EXT. BROWN HOUSE – NIGHT

Establishing shot.

190 INT. BROWNS' PARLOR – NIGHT

Jake and Holt sleep side-by-side on the floor. Sweat dapples Jake's brow. He tosses, in the midst of a bad dream.

He bolts awake, disturbing Holt.

HOLT

Can't sleep?

JAKE

Naw, these quilts are too heavy. They make me sweat.

HOLT

Mine, too.

JAKE

Holt? You know, I probably got only one more fight in me – I'm gonna kill Pitt Mackeson, either when he comes here or when I can get up to find him out. You know that, Holt?

HOLT

Yes, I do. And what you gonne do after you kill Pitt? You gonna join up with them regulars?

JAKE

Fight for the cause? What about you?

HOLT

You really askin' me?

(*thinking*)

What cause you think I got? When them Yankees came and killed George's pa and all his brothers and kin, I stood with George Clyde.

JAKE

He was as good a friend to you as Jack Bull was to me.

HOLT

And they's both good and dead, Roedel. They's both good and dead. You know, Roedel, when I was a boy, I pray'd sometimes for the grace of dyin' myself, 'cause only old man death can make a slave boy free. Then with George and me, it was a joy to walk in death's valley with him, 'cause slave and free is equal in dyin', and we was both dyin' sure. But I keep walkin' now, and I feels it ain't right, cause maybe I don't want no *heaven's* freedom – maybe I want to walk the freedom way in *this* here life.

JAKE

I thought that's what George gave you, when he bought you out.

HOLT

It wasn't his to give, Roedel. Nah, I don't right understand it, but it come to the day George Clyde took that Yankee bullet, *that* was when it made me feel the somethin' new.

JAKE

You felt that loss –

HOLT

No! What I felt was diff'rent. What I felt was now – now I was gonna be free. Oh that George Clyde – I loved him sure. But being his friend was no diff'rent from being his nigger – and Roedel – I never, never again gonna be nobody's nigger.

Holt rolls over and the conversation ends.

125

191 EXT. BROWNS' HOUSE. PORCH – DAY

Jake looks out over the fields. He sees Holt at work side-by-side with Orton and Sue Lee. Sue Lee stops her work and walks towards the house.

The baby is at his feet. She scuttles across the floor and he walks stiffly toward her – his leg obviously mending.

Sue Lee enters. Without a word she picks the child up and sits down in the rocking-chair.

Jake positions himself at her feet.

The show begins.

192 INT. BROWNS' HOUSE. PARLOR – DAY

Morning. Holt and Jake are still on the floor, though Jake has awakened and is rising, as Orton walks from his bedroom with his boots, still sleepy-eyed.

> ORTON
>
> How you feelin', Dutchy?

> JAKE
>
> Not so bad.

> ORTON
>
> You look like you feel right good. You feel good?

> JAKE
>
> I don't feel too bad.

> ORTON
>
> Aw, you seem about healed up to me.

> JAKE
>
> It still hurts some, my leg does.

Orton goes to the kitchen, and comes back quickly, gnawing on a piece of bread.

> ORTON
>
> I got to go to Hartwell today. I should be back by night.

126

JAKE

Want me to come along?

ORTON

Naw, you go on and finish healing. I'll take Holt with me, though. He's a handy gunman, I hear tell.

JAKE

That's right.

Orton walks out. Jake awakens Holt.

Holt. Holt. Mr Brown wants you to ride with him to Hartwell.

HOLT

What? All right.

He rises and pulls his boots on. Orton returns with a shotgun.

ORTON

Now you stay here and get your rest, son.

JAKE

I guess I'll do that.

Orton and Holt depart. Jake watches them go.

193 INT. BROWNS' PARLOR – DAY

Jake sits and watches Sue Lee nurse.

SUE LEE

Are you always going to stare like that?

JAKE

Long as I can.

SUE LEE

Well, you're pretty near well, so it won't be much longer. I reckon you and Holt'll be off to get shot by some *different* fellows here pretty soon.

JAKE

Maybe I won't.

SUE LEE

What will you do then?

JAKE

Oh, well maybe I'll trek me on over to California and catch me a sailboat to somewhere sunny.

SUE LEE

Is that right? What grand spot have you got in mind, Jake?

JAKE

Sparta. In Sparta they have olives. I got that out of a book. I could eat me some olives.

SUE LEE

Olives? What are olives like?

JAKE

Well, I don't know first-hand. I never had one yet. But I've ate a bushel of walnuts, and nothin' can be more trouble to eat than them.

(*pause*)

SUE LEE

I wonder about me. I ain't going sailing nowhere, and I know it.

JAKE

Oh, you'll get by.

(*beat*)

You know, that girl needs her a daddy.

SUE LEE

She had a daddy, Jake, and you ain't it.

JAKE

(*rising to his feet*)

You know, girl, you're going to have to get your water from the nearest well, or else learn to love lugging that heavy bucket of yours.

And with that he goes outside.

194 EXT. BROWNS' HOUSE PORCH – DAY

Jake walks out on to the porch.

> JAKE
>
> Damn!

195 INT. BROWN HOUSE – DAY

Jake re-enters to find the parlor empty. He looks over into the dining room, and sees Wilma preparing a chicken for the oven.

> JAKE
>
> A chicken, Wilma, and this ain't Sunday even. What's with the special favors?

> WILMA
>
> Why, nothing. I just know Orton will be mighty tired tonight when he gets back from his ride. I intend to feed him well.

She takes the chicken back into the kitchen.

196 EXT. BROWN HOUSE – EVENING

Jake is perched by the window. He sees Orton and Holt ride up in the company of a fat, pale, dark-dressed stranger. They dismount and quickly enter the house.

They seem grim-faced and determined. Orton holds the shotgun with the butt rested against his leg, pointed down, but ready to rise.

> STRANGER
>
> Is this the man?

> ORTON
>
> That's him. Dutchy Roedel.

> JAKE
>
> What is this?

> ORTON
>
> This is Reverend Horace Wright. You're gettin' married today, Dutchy. You're gettin' married or you're gettin' out.

Holt can barely hold down his sniggering.

JAKE

I'm what?

ORTON

You heard me. You're all healed. I wanted to be sure you wouldn't die slow before I did this. I can't have it in my house the way it is.

Wilma bustles Sue Lee into the room.

JAKE

Holt, saddle my horse. We're gettin' out of here.

HOLT

Oh, no. You should do right, Jake.

JAKE

What on earth does that mean?

Sue Lee gives Jake a poke and points to the front porch.

SUE LEE

Let's talk.

REVEREND WRIGHT

I do believe that is a roasting chicken I smell.

197 EXT. BROWNS' PORCH – EVENING

They walk on to the porch.

Silence.

SUE LEE

Are you going to or not?

JAKE

It's being shoved down my throat. If a thing has got to be shoved, *I* like to do the shoving.

SUE LEE

Okay. Then get on in there and shove, Jake.

Jake sits down.

JAKE

I thought you said you wouldn't want me for a wagonload of
gold 'cause I'm a nubbin-fingered runt of a Dutchman. I
remember you saying that.

SUE LEE
(*sitting beside him*)

Well, I guess I lied.

JAKE

Are you lying again now?

SUE LEE

No. I wouldn't lie to you, Jake.

JAKE

You just told me you lied to me before.

SUE LEE

That's different. That was romance.

Jake pauses over that one.

JAKE

And now is what?

She touches his cheek.

SUE LEE

Now is the truth. This here now is the truth.

JAKE

Jack Bull would want that girl to have a daddy. He was like a
brother. I guess I'll do it.

SUE LEE

I guess you will.

198 INT. BROWNS' PARLOR – NIGHT

The Reverend mumbles through the ceremony.

REVEREND WRIGHT

You, Jacob Friedrich Roedel, being the man, take you, Sue
Lee Shelley Jackson, being the woman, so that by the power
vested in me you two are right married.

131

ORTON

Ain't it so!

Holt slaps Jake on the back as the Reverend heads to the table to check out dinner.

SUE LEE

That sure was a fast ceremony.

JAKE

I reckon that man would marry stones to stones if there was a chicken at the end of it.

ORTON

That's neither here nor somewhere else. He done made you legal.

199 INT. BROWNS' DINING ROOM – NIGHT

The food is being mopped up and the last of many toasts is given. Sue Lee is also drinking. She clinks her glass with Holt's.

200 INT. BROWNS' PARLOR – NIGHT

Orton says goodnight to Jake and Holt and closes his bedroom door.

Jake and Holt pick up their bedding and walk into the parlor, only to look down on the floor to see the Reverend, asleep and snoring, taking up their usual spot. The Reverend has a number of pistols on him.

Holt gathers his blanket.

> HOLT
> You a family man now. How do you feel?

Jake grabs his blanket, and sits next to him on the floor.

> JAKE
> I feel the same, Holt. Hell, it's only words.

> HOLT
> No, it's a oath, Jake. That's words that you got to back up.

> JAKE
> Oh, I know that. I reckon we'll be haulin' her and the kid with us now.

> HOLT
> Where to?

> JAKE
> I don't know. What do you think of California?

Holt watches him with a puzzled look as he takes his boots off and lies next to him.

> HOLT
> What you doing?

> JAKE
> What am I doing? Have you gone blind? I am going to sleep. I am fixing to get me some sleep.

> HOLT
> (*shaking his head*)
> Jake. Do I got to tell you this?

133

JAKE

Tell me what?

HOLT

You *s'posed* to sleep with the wife, Jake. For pity sake, you got to know that much. You s'posed to share her bed, that way some other man do that you shoot him.

JAKE

I know all that. You bet I know that. But hell, this ain't some regular marriage situation.

HOLT

Don't you like her? You ain't gonna lie to me that you don't.

JAKE

I like her. She's pretty enough and all that. But this marriage thing has swept up kind of all the sudden.

HOLT

Well, Jake, it *is* over you. I mean to say, you done the milkin', you might as well have the cream.

Jake thinks for a moment, gets up and grabs his boots.

201 INT. SUE LEE'S ROOM – NIGHT

Jake cautiously goes to the door, and slowly opens it. Sue Lee is lying in bed, her eyes closed, a candle lit nearby.

The baby is asleep in a small crib on wheels.

As he steps in, she opens her eyes.

SUE LEE

Jake.

She sits up in bed, her cotton gown leaving her shoulders bare.

Jake goes to the bedside, puts his boots and pistols down, fumbles with the button on his britches, then gives up and starts into bed.

Hey, take your clothes off. You don't come to bed in dirty duds, Jake. Now that's a rule.

JAKE
(*standing*)

Just how many rules is it you've got lined up for me, girl?

SUE LEE

Oh, don't get mad.

She gets out of bed, her gown nearly transparent. She takes the crib and pushes it into the hall, then closes the door behind her.

Here, I'll help you.

She pulls his shirt over his head, then sits on the bed and unbuttons his britches. They drop to the floor.

She smiles.

Hmm.

She takes her gown off, and lays back, naked, on the bed.

He stands there and looks.

SUE LEE

Are you virgin?

JAKE

I've sinned plenty.

SUE LEE

But have you ever bedded a woman before?

JAKE

Girl, I've killed fifteen men.

SUE LEE
(*laughing*)

Come here.

He lies down. She rolls him over and gets on top of him. They kiss.

202 EXT. BROWNS' FARM – DAY

Jake and Holt are finishing the repair of a wagon, stretching canvas over hoops of wood.

Orton and Sue Lee come up.

135

JAKE

Ort, I mean it. You and Wilma should be riding with us. The war's comin' here any day now.

ORTON

I suppose. But this is home. And, besides, there's a lot of bad sorts between here and California. I reckon if you ain't shot *for* a thief you'll be shot *by* a thief.

203 INT. BROWNS' HOUSE. SUE LEE'S ROOM – NIGHT

Jake, Sue Lee and the baby asleep.

The low rumble of horse hooves begins to be heard.

Jake stirs, gets out of bed, puts his pants on, grabs his pistols and exits.

204 INT. BROWNS' HOUSE PARLOR – NIGHT

Holt is already up and by the window, gun drawn. The sound of the riders increases, then fades.

He and Jake look at each other.

205 EXT. BROWNS' HOUSE – DAY

Orton rides up, dismounts.

206 INT. BROWNS' HOUSE. DINING ROOM – DAY

The men are gathered at the dining-room table.

ORTON

Newport's full of militia. They chased Dave Pool and another gang into the woods behind Virgil Clement's place. Killed four of 'em.
                    (*beat*)
Jake – Pitt Mackeson's about. And he knows you're here. I can't say as if it's more dangerous to stay or to go.

SUE LEE
                    (*standing in the doorway*)
We'll go tomorrow.

136

Jake nods his head.

207 INT. BROWNS' HOUSE PARLOR – NIGHT

Jake and Holt stand watch.

Holt turns to Jake.

> HOLT
> Jake, I do a lot for you, you know that?

> JAKE
> You know I do. It's equal.

> HOLT
> Oh, don't say it, Jake. I got a thing to say.

> JAKE
> All right.

> HOLT
> Jake, I'll travel with you and yours 'til we travel past them Pin
> Indians and riffraff in the Nation, then I got to go off somewhere.

> JAKE
> Where? Where will you go?

> HOLT
> I ain't decided that to a definite aim. But I'm going. I'm
> going to find my mama. I believe she was sold to Texas, so
> that is where I will begin. If she was sold there, I will go there
> and pay to buy her freedom.

> JAKE
> Holt, you done already paid more than enough to buy that.

> HOLT
> I hear you.

> JAKE
> I wish you well, Holt.

> HOLT
> It ain't yet. I ain't leavin' you 'til your little Dutch ass is past
> Pitt Mackeson and them Pin Indians. I told you that, didn't I.

JAKE

Yes, you did.

208 EXT. BROWNS' PORCH – DAY

Jake sits in a chair in the middle of the parlor as Orton cuts his hair.

JAKE

Goodbye Bushwhacker curls.

ORTON

Dutchy, you look twenty-one again.

JAKE

I'm just now nineteen, Ort.

ORTON

Oh, is that right? Well, you'll never look that young.

Jake looks at his hair as it falls around him, wistful.

JAKE
(*to Holt*)

I said I'd never cut my hair 'til I was finished with the war.

HOLT

And you didn't, Jake. You didn't.

209 EXT. BROWNS' FARM – DAY

Holt and Jake carefully place their guns in the back of the wagon, under a blanket.

ORTON

Militia finds those, you're not too likely to get farther than the nearest hangin' tree.
(*as Jake grabs the reins*)
Hell, good luck, y'all.

Orton slaps the team and Jake, Holt, Sue Lee and the baby are off.

Wilma cries as she shouts goodbye. Sue Lee waves goodbye from the wagon.

210 EXT. ROAD NEAR NEWPORT — DAY

The wagon, with Holt accompanying it on horseback, struggles along past a crossroads. In front of a storehouse lounges a group of Federal soldiers. They eye the passing family disinterestedly. Jake and Holt keep their eyes on the road.

211 EXT. CREEKSIDE — DAY

The team is being watered. Jake starts a small fire under a kettle behind the wagon.

Holt cautiously scans the creekside opposite.

From the woods behind them, two figures on horseback emerge nonchalantly. It's a smiling Pitt Mackeson, a half-dozen scalps hanging from his bridle, and a dejected Turner Rawls.

> PITT MACKESON
> Why, Dutchy, I didn't expect to see you no more.

Jake and Holt stand, weaponless and speechless. Pitt's fingers play lightly over one of his many revolvers, but he doesn't draw.

> JAKE
> Howdy, Pitt. Turner.

> TURNER
> Howdy.

> JAKE
> Water is boiling. You like some chicory?

Sue Lee clasps the baby.

> PITT
> I think I will. I think I'd like some chicory, Dutchy. How you, Holt?

Jake makes his way gingerly to the rear of the wagon, where he begins to prepare the chicory. We can see his eyes dart occasionally at where he has stored his guns.

> HOLT
> Fairly well.

JAKE

Are you two alone?

TURNER

Just us now. We been on the run – sort of constant.

JAKE

How is Black John?

PITT

That's a big question, Dutchy, 'cause the man is dead. Black
John is dead. And who ain't? They got him at Dover and
stuck his head on a pole and paraded it down the streets.
They put a picture of it in their paper.
(looking right at Jake)
Quantrill too – over the river. It's been rough times for them
who stuck it out.

JAKE

Aw, the war is lost.

PITT

No shit, Dutchy. Who does this gal and kid belong to?

JAKE

That's my wife.

PITT

Huh, if that don't beat all. You got a wife.

JAKE

Where you headed?

*Jake walks to Pitt and Turner, who remain atop their horses, and
carefully hands them their cups of chicory.*

PITT

Newport.

JAKE

Hell, man. There's two hundred Federals in Newport. We
just rode through 'em. You won't be able to go in there.

PITT

Wrong, Dutchy. I *am* going in there. I'm for certain sure

140

goin' in there. I want a drink. And they have drinks in
Newport.

*Jake goes back to the boiling water, positioning himself ever closer to the
back of the wagon.*

> JAKE

They'll kill you. You'd best stay clear out of there.

> PITT

I don't think so, Dutchy. I don't reckon I'll clear out of where
I was born. That there was my hometown, and I reckon I'll
go on in and have me a drink there.

> JAKE

Turner, you too?
> (*Turners nods yes*)
They'll kill you sure.

> PITT

Oh, oh. What a horrible fate. Haw, haw. Yes, a horrible fate.

*Jake swiftly reaches into the back of the wagon and pulls a rifle, aiming
it at Pitt.*

Pitt raises his hands in the air, not even attempting to draw

> (*laughing*)

Dutchy, old boy! You got me now! Oh boy!

His laughter turns almost maniacal.

> TURNER

Jake?

Jake just stands aiming the gun at Pitt.

> PITT

C'mon, Turner.

*Pitt, still laughing, kicks his horse and moves back up the wooded lane.
Turner, a last anxious look at Holt and Jake, follows.*

> (*without looking back*)

So long, boys. We'll raise our glasses to you in Newport!

(*to Jake, whose rifle follows Pitt's back*)
You gonna shoot him?

Jake looks at Holt, then over to Sue Lee. She looks deeply into his eyes.

The horsemen spur their horses and ride swiftly away.

Jake, trembling, still points the gun in their direction, then lets it drop.

That's right, Jake.

JAKE
It ain't right and it ain't wrong. It just is.

He walks back to the wagon and tosses the rifle in. Holt and Sue Lee watch him.

212 EXT. HIGH PLAINS – DAY

In a small grove planted in the midst of a vast expanse of open prairie, the wagon sits in the glow of the day's first sunlight.

Inside the wagon, Sue Lee sleeps with the baby in her arms. Jake gently pulls himself out of the wagon.

Holt is sitting on the ground with his pistols spread out before him. He places each one carefully in his pockets and belt. His horse is saddled and ready to go.

JAKE
It's now?

Holt nods.

You certain you want to ride – with your guns like that?

Holt rises, nods silently again.

They walk together to the back of the wagon.

Let me wake 'em, Holt.

HOLT
No Jake, you let them sleep. You know I ain't much for goodbyes. But – I'll just tip my hat.

JAKE

Sure.

Holt peers inside at the sleeping woman and baby.

He touches the brim of his hat.

He walks to his horse, but before he mounts it, he takes Jake's hand.

Daniel Holt.

HOLT

Jacob Roedel.

Jake smiles bravely as Holt mounts his horse, tips his hat, and turns.

From afar, we see Holt ride off, heading south, as Jake stands by the wagon and watches him.